ALIVE IN CHRIST

The Gift

Christ Speaks Series
Volume 1

Alive in Christ, *The Gift*
Volume 1 of the *Christ Speaks* Series

Copyright © 2011, 2017, 2018, 2019 All for Zion.
All rights reserved.

Fourth Edition 2019, with various corrections to the text.

All rights reserved. No part of this book may be reproduced in any form or by any means without permission in writing from the publisher, All for Zion.

For additional copies of this book or information on other books and materials, visit:

www.ChristSpeaks.info

All for Zion
P.O. Box 256
Fairview, Utah 84629

ISBN 13: 978-0-9882977-5-3   ISBN-10: 0-9882977-5-2

Fourth Edition
Printed in the United States of America by
Peczuh Printing, Lindon, Utah
10 9 8 7 6 5 4 3 2 1

Table of Contents

Preface v

Editor's Comments vi

Rejoice and Receive! ix

Chapter 1 The Gift 1
   Being Alive in Christ 2
   Unifying the Spirit with the Physical Body 6

Chapter 2 The Vibrations of Thoughts 13
   The Value of Sacred Time 17
   Inspired Living 19

Chapter 3 Your True Divine Nature 25
   Born into Greater Glories 28
   Future New World 34

Chapter 4 Experience Divine Nature 37
   Sacred Prayer Time 37
   Power of Spirit in Words 46

Chapter 5 Spirit Gives You Life 49
   Restoring Divine Peace 51
   Walk Forward in Prayer 57

Chapter 6 Life Path, Life Plan 59
   Being Away for Learning 59
   Life Plans and Resurrection 64

Chapter 7 Eternalness While On Earth 69
   Overcoming Death for the New World 71
   Humility and Surrendering to God's Will 76

Chapter 8 The Keys of Love, Gratitude, and Praise 79
   Feeling the Presence of God's Spirit 80
   How You Multiply Spiritual Energy 87

Chapter 9 I Will Come and Be Before You 89
   Your Being is to Be a Portal to Heaven 92
   My Invitation for You 95

My Request **101**

Chapter 10 Ultimate Spiritual Awareness **103**
    Developing Your Spiritual Awareness *104*
    Maintain the Love Factor *109*

Chapter 11 Respectful, Honest Conversation **115**
    Clarifying Your Responsibility *120*
    My Invitation to You *129*

Chapter 12 My Atonement's Infinite Reach **131**
    Your Ultimate Physical Body *133*
    Let Me Become Your Prophet *138*

Chapter 13 Making Truth Permanent **147**
    All Truth Is Connected *149*
    Know Me—Know Truth *157*

Chapter 14 A New Way **161**
    Becoming Aware *162*
    Five Significant Aspects *170*

Chapter 15 Developing the Zion Way **175**
    A Higher Way, an Expansive, Freeing Way *176*
    Create with Me *182*

Chapter 16 This Dispensation is Your Mission **189**
    Current Dispensation's Unique Mission *193*
    Miracles *202*

Chapter 17 Prayer of the Spirit **205**
    The Miracle of the Quiet Place *208*
    A Blessing from the Lord *212*

Final Remarks - Concluding Request **214**

Paragraph Headings Index **217**

Preface

I am Jesus, the Christ, who speaks to you through these written words. What you hold in your hands is not just a book but a singular treasure, a personal *Gift* I offer you out of my love for you and my intimate knowing of you. This message from Me to you is set with a blessing upon it to move you from just reading words to having a life-changing experience, if you will let it.

I have commissioned the writing of this message because this is the time upon the Earth when My clear instructions must come forth to give birth of a new world, a world prepared to receive Me. I come soon. For this very purpose, I have opened up the necessary *Gifts of the Spirit* within the precious, humble disciple through whom I relay this message. This entire endeavor is under My supervision and direction.

The fulfillment intended for you cannot be accomplished if you read this as you would any other book. This is not intended just to relay information. It is intended to touch your spirit and enliven your whole being. Every time I repeat something, it is because you need again to be fed the spirit of those words. It is not because you did not read and understand them before. Like the constant nourishment needed for your bodies in which you eat the same food many times, your spirit needs to be fed and nourished by truth again and again, even though you fully digested and gained value from the previous time.

Do not read with the intention just to find out what is said, but instead thoughtfully read every portion; ponder each part carefully, even each sentence. Please read this with prayer every time you begin. With every piece of information ask yourself how it can apply to your life.

Ask what validity this material holds for you. Invite Me to be interactive with your thoughts. When I ask you to stop in the middle of a section to pray or receive a blessing, please do so. Do not rush through this. Read this slowly and conscientiously. The pattern of the world and a tool of Satan is to rush, but living in haste will divert you from your true path Divinely set for your life.

Much of the message will not be new to you, though some of it will be. However, all is intended to be felt and received anew and to bring life and empowerment into you from each thought.

I so desire for you to know Me personally. I desire you to receive the *Gift* from the Atonement I have for you, to understand it and to become fully Alive in Me. Even right now ask for a blessing from Me, and I will bring vitality into these words so this message will be the life-changing experience I have intended this to be for you.

Editor's Comments

This is the first volume in a series of books delivered in power and beauty by Jesus the Christ. His message is for those who deeply desire to be one with Our Redeemer and who are sincerely seeking for 'further light and knowledge' and an understanding of how to create Zion within.

Zion is being established in these end times preparatory to our Lord's glorious Second Coming. This coming forth of Zion requires a people who are willing to set their hearts upon a whole new way of being. It requires them to become of one heart and one mind, with one another, and with Christ and our God. Have you ever wondered how this pure way of living is to be established? How will the Lord prepare a people who are truly of one heart and one mind? Do we need to work harder? Be more obedient?

The answer to these questions may surprise you. They open up beautiful new insights into Christ's redeeming grace, which is more profound, greater, and more personal than most people truly realize. Among other things, the process includes coming to know, without a doubt, that you are a pure-in-heart divine child of Heavenly Parents advancing to become a Zion person who, in the process, is overcoming the fallen nature of this earth to rise to a exquisite new way of being.

The Gift
In this volume, The Lord presents you with a *Gift* and teaches not only this process of creating Zion within, but also becoming one with Him through a deeper and more sacred personal relationship. He also expands upon the pure, cherishing Love that God and Divine Beings have for each one of us, and how keenly aware and involved They are in our lives. He also explains our part in acquiring and developing a soul with a deep, unchangeable testimony of all Truth and how we can reclaim our true divine natures.

Faithful Transcription
This text has been taken from a recorded revelation from Christ. This written format is not a word-for-word tran-

scription, though the original spirit and power of the oral message have been carefully and faithfully preserved on every level in these written words. All has been carefully done with the Lord's constant, guiding direction.

Lord's Way of Teaching

In our earthly culture, a common format for written material is linear, a straight line from point to point until the conclusion is reached. The Lord's way of teaching often uses repetition and extension of thoughts looping back to the original point, somewhat resembling the pattern of a daisy. The center is the main idea; the overlapping petals are like the supporting information presented in loops. The purpose of this format is to reinforce the original concept while adding on small expansions with each loop. This daisy-like format strengthens the central point for the reader and expands his or her understanding.

Liberal Capitalization

In the text, liberal capitalization is used in referring to Deity: Heavenly Parents, Mother, Father, etc. This is done not only to show reverence but also to help clarify the reference to Godhood. Some descriptive words, such as Divine Nature, Holy, and Eternal, which also refer to Deity, are capitalized. Also, the pronouns that refer to only Deity are capitalized: Us, We, He, Our, etc. The pronouns that refer to the combination of Christ and the reader use lower case: we, us, our, etc. We trust this will help clarify.

It is our sincere hope and belief that you, the reader will be as profoundly touched by this life-changing book as we have been.

The Editors

Rejoice and Receive!

Oh dear reader, rejoice! Receive this further light upon relationships as they have been and how glorious and empowering they may now become!

Open wide your spirit! Receive now more of that which you have hungered for and thirsted after—more details, more depth of understanding, more knowledge-pure and whole, more unveiling of the profoundly personal nature of Christ's atoning *Gift* that has claimed you His!

As you read the words and comprehend the message being so lovingly imparted, may your thirsty soul drink in that which you have desired, and wondered about, and thought upon, and longed for, but have not known where to find it. With a continual prayer to our Holy Parents above, unlatch the doors of your heart! Open wide the windows of your beautiful mind! Breathe in the life-giving air of added truth! Receive this fresh fount of His precious, living water! This is the *Gift* being offered to you in this wondrous way. Let us become so **Alive!**

Raphael and Rachael

This book is dedicated to

Jesus the Christ

AND TO THE BUILDING OF ZION
FOR
THE MESSIAH'S SECOND COMING

~ With All Glory to God ~

Chapter 1

The Gift

I am Jesus, the Christ, who writes this book with a particular, time-sensitive purpose. This writing is intended to be a direct communication from Me to you, personally. I am calling out to you, My humble follower, asking you to come and know Me fully. Preparing to know Me personally can only be accomplished through the *full* embracing of My Atonement. To obtain the greater glory of exaltation, you must choose to completely engage with Me in the application of the Atonement in your life. I am knocking at your door right now. Please, let Me in. I invite you to know Me personally as your Friend; let Me walk with you in every moment. Come, let us begin now!

My message in this book is vitally important and of infinite worth to you. It is My prayer—literally My holy supplication—that you receive what I have to give with a feeling that stirs your heart and that you understand My words differently than you ever have before. Every time you read this, I desire for you to hear and feel My words anew. Let the reading of this book be woven with much prayer. Read this carefully and slowly; We do not rush in the Heavens. Be pensive. I ask you even now to pause and talk to Me through prayer. Even now lay down this book and let's talk.

There are some things I would have you come to know that I have not shared in such openness before and to the degree I am today. This expanded awareness is absolutely necessary for you to be truly alive in Me.

As you read through this book, it may seem at times that the same message is being repeated. There is a purpose in that. My desire is that you be open and be prayerful *every* time you read this message—again and again. I ask you to open your heart in prayer; open your mind's understanding with your spirit's awakened senses through communication with Me to influence your whole being.

There may be many things taught here you have heard before; however, I will also give additional perceptions and I will witness through My spirit what I am sharing. I greatly desire for you to *experience* what I teach and I will open up personal experiences in your life to support what I am giving to you.

Being *Alive in Christ*

What does it mean to be *Alive in Christ*? I have created a holy Gift which few have opened to the fullest extent. The purpose of this message is to invite you to experience the Gift of My Atonement to the fullest capacity. There are different beliefs about the Atonement, but for the most part, people do not know what completely happened, why it was necessary, what it means, where the

Chapter 1 - The Gift

Atonement took place, or even that it is to be used in every moment.

I will share further what did occur during the Atonement so you will understand it more and how it applies in your life *right now*. The Atonement is more than forgiving sins, being resurrected, living beyond the physical body's death, and dwelling in the Heavens for eternity. My Atonement offers *much, much* more.

In this holy, sacred time which took place while I was in the Garden of Gethsemane, I was transported spiritually into another dimension of time and reality. Though it was relatively short in the number of Earth's hours, time was extended for Me, and I was given the ability to comprehend past, present, and future so I could fully experience the life of everyone for whom I was atoning. Because the fullness of God, the Father, was in Me, My physical body had capacities to do things that are not possible in a mortal body. Though His Essence was in Me and His Nature present in My physical form, His complete Holiness had not yet been *expanded* in My body until I finalized the full receiving of His Gift to Me which took place during the Atonement.

While in Gethsemane, I was allowed an intimate connection to the life of each individual who had or would live on Earth. It was as if each person stood personally before Me, and I was allowed to have all of their experiences infused into My being. In this different dimension, I was allowed to live your life—to know every experience, every thought, every emotion, every struggle, every triumph, and everything you have felt or will yet feel in your physical body; I experienced your life as you are experiencing it now.

As I did so, with the perfection of the Father within Me, I was allowed to bring forth a balancing and alignment of your life to Eternal Truth. I brought forth the understanding for everything not understood. Every error you made was corrected, whether it was by conscious choice, in innocence, or not knowing a better alternative. Whether you call it sin, error, mistake, or weakness, all was made perfect. I was allowed to take all that is imperfect in your physical body, all ailments, deformities, sickness, and poor health and bring forth perfection for your physical form. I created exalted perfection for your physical body to be united with your spirit being. I offer you a perfected body and soul, so you can be like our Holy Father in Heaven, even as I am, for I have the fullness of the Father in Me. This is what I offer to you; *this is My Gift, your Exalted and Eternal Life which is the fulfillment of My Atonement.*

God literally fathered My body. His energy, His power, His very structure was and is in Me, and with His Light and Nature I have created your life in perfection. The transferring of the nature of His perfected physical form and the fullness of all that He is that exists in Me has been prepared to be transferred to you. I offer to transform your physical form as if God had directly been the father of your body. This Gift of *All* the Father is, as if

Chapter 1 - The Gift

suspended in time, is waiting for you to accept. It is a step-by-step, moment by moment realization.

I am asking for you to come in prayer; I will expand your faith to receive this Gift I am offering you. We are to work daily to bring forth a deliverance of each portion of perfection, as it is needed, for the development in your physical being and spiritual exaltation. It is not possible to deliver the fullness of your perfection in one moment. Your body could not adjust that quickly. But each day was designed with the ultimate and highest of possibilities. Come. Come in holy prayer. Come with a desire that every day be at its absolute peak of excellence. I am here to deliver to you the maximum amount of the Divine Ways that you can receive in each moment, so you may grow as if you are in a womb.

Born Again

You have heard the term to be Born Again. There are different levels of this, and as the term indicates, there is a newness of life. In a true Born Again experience, you significantly leave behind any unrighteous ways, and, step by step, embrace a new, holier, expanded life. As you move from one level of Light and Glory to the next, a process of being Born Anew takes place each time. The ultimate is to be *born* into the highest of glories and be like our Heavenly Parents. These birthing processes are part of the greatest blessings of My Atonement for you.

The *ultimate* Born Again progression is for your body to be changed *as if you had been born of God's body*. The Divine genetics are transferred through Me to you, and you literally become a co-heir with Me to the Father. I have been given the holy position of being the new Father, or the Mediator, to transfer all that the Father gave to Me to you as you learn to accept the fullness of what each day can be for you. The ultimate intention can be for you to receive the maximum of God's Glory[1] during this phase of your existence.

Regardless of what state of deterioration your physical body may be in, you are preparing it to receive the fullness of its perfect form, function, and capacities, even such divine capacities beyond what is normally experienced in this physical world. This happens when the higher powers are infused into it. There will be continual progression and additional lessons after you have parted this world, whether through death and resurrection or by your mortal life being transformed and extended by Me.

Unifying the Spirit with the Physical Body

After death and during the life review, a person's spirit-being decides which patterns of the physical body will be kept. All physical bodies have incorporated incorrect, de-

---

[1] **Glory** is the Divine Light that emanates from perfected God Beings holding the perfect balance and harmony of Divine Masculine and Divine Feminine.

Light is the holy spiritual substance that comes from the combined energies of Love and Truth. Human beings emanate Light, a spiritual essence similar to the light from the sun, only more refined. Only the Light coming from perfected God Beings is Glory—glorified Light.

teriorating patterns from the person's own misperceptions and the inherited fallen nature, the false teachings of this world and energetic influences of Satan. These patterns need to be converted and changed in order for life to continue eternally. The new patterns will be placed into your body with My assistance which is a key part of the resurrection's fulfillment. Your physical body is sacred and ultimately will go with you for eternity.

After death, people have a fuller perspective and greater understanding of the realities and experiences of this earth life. Each person decides strictly by personal choice just what patterns, habits, abilities, personality traits experienced in this physical life they would like to keep and have sealed permanently. Never is there force, pressure, or coercion to choose a certain way. Even in the Heavens, you have choice. Once the decisions have been made, I infuse a sealing of these qualities into the spirit body and prepare a match of patterns to be put into the physical body. There must be a harmony and unity between the physical body and the spirit body for resurrection to take place. Again, these are each person's personal decisions, and God always honors the decisions.

Making life review decisions is possible while your spirit is still in your physical body. In other words, it is possible for you to make new decisions now and work with Me to start the 'resurrection' process or in other words, the raising up and restoring of your divine nature. It is actually easier to make the changes while in your physical body. I realize you have the influencing energies of the fallen world, but with Me, you can completely draw away from that energy until it is no longer an influence. The Atonement is not just for your life hereafter; *the Atonement is for everyday application now.* This idea is one of the major teachings I want you to understand.

The bodies of Adam and Eve were designed in the likeness and holy form of God. Their bodies began in a state of excellence. Because of Satan, the deceiving one, his nature came upon and into the bodies of Adam and Eve. As a result, all bodies since then have been impacted by Satan's deceptions and lies. Two patterns and influences exist in the body. One is the distorted energy of Satan, the fallen nature, which causes the decline of the body unto death. The second pattern and influence is the Divine energy and form of Godliness, which creates and sustains life. When yielded to and with My Atonement power, this Divine energy pattern moves one toward the opportunity of perfection of Eternal Life.

If it weren't for My Atonement, this decline of the body would cause the death of the spirit body also, but your spirit is shielded and protected by the Atonement. That is part of the promise I made to you and the plan of God the Father, even before this Earth began. Everyone's spirit will continue after death. With the resurrection, I will infuse life back into the physical form, and all bodies will be lifted up, entirely restored[2] and will continue on

---

[2] Sometimes people ask about a physical body that has been completely altered from its form. I know the substance and matter, and will reform and

Chapter 1 - The Gift

until they are ready to completely receive all Holy, Divine, Eternal Truth, and embrace and live it fully. At least this is one way.

Some, however, will not go through a death because their mortal bodies will be changed and transformed before death instead. Some will stay on this world, remaining alive in their transformed or translated bodies. Oh, dear one, I invite you to realize that *much more can be done* when you choose to hold firm with real intent and apply the Atonement in each moment of every day. My Atonement is not just for the end of your life or just to erase errors and sins; it is for an everyday application! This daily application will strengthen you to act in your most ideal capacity.

You may receive the *fullness* of the Gift of the Atonement while in this life. In order for this to take place, I must completely unite your spirit with your physical being, wholly unifying together all of your being with My holy power and energies while you are yet in the physical body. I invite you to come and learn more and draw closer to Me so we can accomplish the greatest of achievements I have carefully prepared for you! Come and be fully alive in Me!

---

restore all the elements that have been in a physical body. Any deformities that were in the body, even in the original formation in the womb, will be formed perfectly, and all beings will be beautiful.

Misunderstandings

Many of the ideas you have been taught are incomplete truths and have distortions, misunderstandings, and false definitions. Not only will I empower you to live the things you presently believe, but I also offer the opportunity to correct, complete, clarify, and add accurate interpretations to your present understandings. This does not mean the words were not delivered purely in the beginning. Even My holy prophets' words have been misinterpreted and misunderstood.

Words have false definitions or meanings attached to them. Original meanings have become corrupted because this world is filled with the spirit of dishonesty that exists in everyone to some degree unless they have been purified by Me. Some people yield to the false teachings, and some people do not—at least not as much. Yet all have fallen short of completely adhering only to what God would pour forth into them because they have lived in a body and a culture with corruption.

My intention is to invite you to understand how you and I can have a closer relationship, clear the false perceptions and definitions, and turn to a truer understanding. This can really only take place by divine personal inspiration and revelation. This is what I am offering to you. Again, I say to you, come; come and be with Me. Come to know Me and let us have a close, personal relationship. This is what I so desire!

Chapter 1 - The Gift

I understand you may have sought diligently for this connection. You may or may not feel sure about the divine inspiration that comes to you. If you desire to hear My holy words and revealed truth and receive the Gifts of the Spirit, there are certain steps in making you ready. I am prepared to deliver to you each day a small part of your absolute, exalted, and eternal perfection, which is *uniquely designed just for you* to fit specifically with your life.

You might be very intent on receiving My Gift in a certain manner. You might have an idea of what you *think* the Born Again experience *should be* like for you. It can be different for each person. Let go of your perception of what such will be like for you. Just trust. I will bring to you this experience and mighty change as you continue on in sincerity.

Also, you might believe you must hear My voice in your mind to be led and guided by Me. Though this is a possibility, sometimes I bring upon you an infusion of energy that is not immediately transferred to your mind in direct words; nevertheless, I have delivered spirit, Light, and truth into your being. This indirect way is sometimes an advantage. If you were to hear My words directly, you could easily take and combine My thoughts with the old definition and even the corrupted, distorted, or incomplete meanings that you already have within you. Instead, the infusion of Light I send will begin to work upon you and gently but steadily help to clear out the false ideas quietly from within. Be patient and believe that I will carefully prepare you and lead you forward in the way that is best for you to grow and learn. Stay diligent. Stay true. Keep coming. I will bring you the new birth. I will open the Gifts of the Spirit that are best for you in the timing and wisdom in Me.

Chapter 2

The Vibrations of Thoughts

I invite all to come unto Me. I am inviting you personally, right now, to come and be with Me. I am sharing several things I hope will be appealing to move you forward in your progression. Again, realize there are many ways I lead you and communicate with you. I may give you direct words in a spirit of revelation, holy conversation, and communication. You are invited to receive or have been given, the Gift of the Holy Ghost to work with you.

As time moves forward, I will be the One to *directly* communicate with you. Our communications may come in words, in vision, impressions, impulses, a physical manifestation, or thoughts brought into your mind. These subtle impressions are promised to everyone. You may also have other extended Gifts of the Spirit which were selected specifically for you because I knew they would be the best way for you to learn.

You have the ability to receive *impressions*. This ability is in your nature. These impressions can be an advantage that goes beyond hearing specific words. When an overall impression or prompting is delivered into your physical being, it also gives you the ability and spiritual power to move forward upon the new action prompted. Perhaps you will have an overall stirring within you that will enable not only your mind to understand something but also your whole being. Your body can be infused with that power and capacity as if I put the thoughts into actions already. You want to have more than just the idea or answer; you want to have the capacity and divine power to act upon and fulfill the idea or answer.

Thoughts are vibrational frequencies that reside in your physical brain and are remembered. I can put the same kind of frequency not only into your mind but into every cell of your physical body, supporting you to respond to My information and inspiration. My impressions can infuse the wholeness of what I would have you feel, know, and act upon. It is an impression of Truth upon your whole physical being that your spirit knows and that I desire to deliver to you at that time.

Some will not believe these impressions are from Divine Source for a variety of reasons. Often a person will simply think these impressions are their own great ideas. Some may consider it is possibly inspired but are concerned that they might be wrong. Others will doubt they are worthy to receive any inspiration and may say: *I cannot. I am not worthy.* Those thoughts are not true. You are worthy in the very fact that you are a divine, holy child of God. Do not make a judgment upon yourself. You are pursuing and looking forward to an increase of your

Chapter 2 - The Vibrations of Thoughts

personal, eternal development and coming closer to Me and your Holy Eternal Mother and Father.

Oft times I give you an impression which is ignored or pushed aside. Begin to act and follow up with the impressions; continue to be prayerful so you can be directed moment by moment. Sometimes an inspired idea is not to be acted upon right away, and you are to continue to pray for the timing and guidance of each step. I may bring the understanding of a principle[3] or teaching to assist you to make a decision. If you are reading scriptures, for example, and you are reading over something that you have heard before with many descriptions, understandings, and definitions, I may place an impression upon you to give you a new awareness.

In that moment your mind suddenly comprehends in a new way, a new angle which could change or even reverse what you understood before. That is inspired revelation and is not just your own logic coming up with a new idea. As you take that new thought and move through your life, you will now have a newly empowered concept to apply to everyday situations.

The Holy Scriptures and modern-day revelations that have been written are all intended to guide, direct, and

---

[3] A Principle of truth is an eternal, *life giving* rule with an accompanying balancing Love Essence virtue that provides the fuel needed to apply the rule—in the moment—to achieve the best outcome in the highest way. "Principles are rearrange-able but not do-away-able."

move you forward until you receive new guidance from the Spirit, personal scriptures for you, your 'new scriptures'! These holy impressions are for every day, even for every moment. I will refine you as you receive these impressions. Often the mind is very eager to take complete control of the situation, and some may resist or restrict receiving inspiration because of wanting to take control and do it 'their way'. There can be fear and worry: *Is it right? What if I am wrong? What if this is false? What if this is from a wrong source?*

Please, dear one, trust. If you have prayed, asked with a sincere desire and pure intent, and have received an impression which leads you to do good, then act upon this. Believe, and I will continue to guide you. Apply your faith. This will become stronger, and you will become sure. Sometimes it is necessary to act upon such or accept the thought before you will *know* that it is Divine inspiration. Ask for fear to be removed. I will send a second witness. I will provide a way for you to know and be sure, step by step, and moment by moment. I will speak to your heart. Trust that I am with you, for this is so, even more than you realize.

Inspired ideas may come from the Holy Ghost or from Me, but the mind wants to take every idea and run it through its filtering system of old thoughts and beliefs and perhaps will say: *Well, this could not possibly be. It does not make sense to me because it does not tie in with what I have been taught before.* Yet I may be asking you to hear the words anew. Listen carefully for it may be exactly what I have taught. Pray to have clarification so you may see that what you are being taught—this new idea—might not be contrary to the ancient teaching at all but *an added expansion of newer and greater understanding.* Truth lives, grows, and expands. Hear things differently and deeper. Hear things more profoundly and more completely. Connect what you have been taught with the new. See in a different manner and connect one idea to another for greater perception.

Then be willing to let go of it all! Yes, that is what I said. Also be *willing* to be wrong—without fear. Be open to receiving from Me over your own will and limited perceptions. Ask again, prayerfully, and I will return the thought to you I am confirming. I will provide a way. Let Me guide you! Let Me teach you! Let Me inspire you! Let Me be with you—always!

The Value of Sacred Time
Take Sacred Time daily—prayerful, contemplative, pondering, and meditative time. This key is absolutely the foundation to greater inspiration and guidance to come forth. I cannot pour impressions into you if you do not open the door. You must do this to advance beyond where you are and beyond the best you can do by yourself! You must be the one that opens up for holy communication. This takes much prayer and time together.

You have been in the habit of directing your life by your mind's logic and thinking or by your emotions and not by the infusion of My Spirit and what your spirit knows. Increased prayer allows the door that has been shut—or only partially opened—to open wide and stay open, so the impressions can come to you throughout the day. Then wisdom can come not just *from* your mind but *into* your mind—from your spirit, the Holy Ghost, and My Spirit—bringing new, purified thoughts, directions, and guidance for everyday actions along with balanced emotions to support you.

Depending on where you are in your progression, sometimes it is necessary to have many prayers throughout the day. These do not need to be long and extensive—though such would also be highly advantageous from time to time. You would greatly benefit by taking a significant portion of time at the beginning and at the end of each day plus have smaller portions of conversations throughout the day. This opens the door wider to move you forward into the new way of living every moment with your spirit's stronger influence and with Divine inspiration.

If you will embrace the *spirit of surrendering,* I will accurately establish the Truth in you and even expand upon it. Be willing to learn anew from My Spirit and inspiration. I am asking you to be *willing* to erase everything, even *your understanding* of scriptures that you have up to now. Then you can read scriptures with new eyes and hear with new ears and gain knowledge by revelation and inspiration. Be willing to read as if these thoughts and ideas have never been read before. Be submissive to Divine and have a willingness to learn 'as a little child'.

This greater power and newness of thought is given to you through holy impressions from your personal spirit, from the Holy Ghost's guidance, and from My Spirit and Light.

As you come each day in prayer with adoration to the Father and sincerely express love, appreciation, and gratitude, the Heavens will respond. God, the Father, immediately returns an infusion of Light into your spirit and your body *every* time you pray. This is without exception. This Divine Light enters *first* through your spirit being and then into your physical being. The more you prayerfully come, the more you allow your spirit to bring into your physical being the infusion of Light to illuminate new thoughts, awareness, guidance, and direction. This Light—a literal divine, spiritual substance—also contains the *fuel and power* to act in righteousness upon those impressions. Your thoughts are then more stimulating, invigorating, inviting, and empowering. You will become alive in Me and begin to receive the greater that I have for you.

Inspired Living

Now your thoughts can have more 'life' to them. Illuminated inspiration and ideas from My Spirit are unlimited in understanding and application. They are living, Light-filled words, thoughts, and impressions bringing forth stimulation to the mind and empowerment to your physical body to act. Your life is intended to be holy and divine with Heavenly guidance bringing joy and peace into every moment.

Even though you are not yet perfected, you can live in a manner to receive the fullness of My Gift constantly for that day. Each moment is to be filled with a continual presence and illumination of peace and joy with beautiful thoughts, guidance, and impressions of what to do, where to go, how to respond, and what to say in all circumstances. This is not a dictated way of living, but supportive, inspired, and enlightened. Keep this firmly in your heart and mind and be constant in pursuing this lofty way of living.

Yes, the ability to live always with Divine's Light starts out small. Increased prayers with the results of greater connections are well worth the joy of living this holy way of life. The daily application allows your spirituality to grow exponentially. Learn to live in this open, connected manner by having holy prayer ideally at the beginning of the day. I realize that you may need to schedule things differently but strive to have ample Sacred Time preferably at the same times every day.

Praise and express your love to the Holy Divine Father and Mother and abundantly express gratitude. *This is the vital foundation.* When pondering about anything, *first* express gratitude and love; *then* ask for enlightenment and assistance. Be open with the faith that you do have. Hold an expectation you will receive, in some manner, the support you need. Every day can be absolutely exhilarating for you. Even though your progress may seem slow, your days will move forward better with ample prayers. Please, My dear one, keep coming. Keep communicating. Keep praying. This new way of living with My Light *continually* will become a joy in every moment. Hear that again—a joy in *every* moment! This is to be—I so desire this for you!

Consistency, Increase, Gratitude, and Praise
A building upon with synergy can take place powerfully when you are consistent in your communication, in your sincere prayers, and in your adoration to the Divine. I tell you, it is important to give that adoration and gratitude in order to open up your 'spiritual door' the widest. If you come in prayer and only ask to receive, the door will only be half open. Open wide by giving gratitude, honor, appreciation, and love to God. You will always get a response when you ask, but when you express love and gratitude, you have a greater capacity to receive whatever God gives forth.

Giving love always prepares you to receive love from God. Amply express your love and gratitude. Make adequate and abundant time every day for praise and worship to God. Yes, then also ask every day to have an infusion of Divine Light to the greatest capacity that you can receive for the day and ask for the things you desire to be brought forth, and this pattern will build one day upon the next.

At first, a measure of Light is delivered, and impressions may come in various ways. They may be subtle, they may be soft, they may be light and not easy to discern at first, but they are there. You might not be sure about these things, but I am asking you to step forward in the application of greater belief and begin to exercise yourself in such to see how it works. Part of your exercise is learning how your physical body—this 'instrument' of yours—works in receiving inspiration, guidance, and direction.

There is nothing wrong with acting upon your impression because in time it will prove to be either Eternal Truth or not. Some people are so fearful of moving forth upon an impression for fear of being wrong. Again, ask to have the fear removed. We do learn best from our experiences. The seed will grow and beautifully become what it is, or it will wither and not bring forth the fruits that you thought it would. Trust. Learn. Grow. I am here to guide you.

Daily application of your efforts and noticing the response that does come are crucial because they build. On a particular day you may receive a certain measure of guidance, inspiration, and infusion of Light. On a later day you will be able to then receive more, say five measures; then it will be fifty measures, and so forth. It can increase and grow by your daily application until there is a great increase within you, a point of experiencing the compounding and exponential growth. You will receive greater infusion of divine impressions upon your conscious mind than you had gained from your own logic and thinking alone. You have been trained by the world's lesser way in which you had to rely on logic rather than divine, spiritual guidance. Ah, dear one, it is so much

Chapter 2 - The Vibrations of Thoughts

greater, so much more joyful and peaceful to live life with the wisdom of Our Father in Heaven added to yours.

You must continue on so that this connection to Light and Heaven's Love will grow rapidly until the greater way of being will be with you. Then all your decisions are made with the empowerment of Love and Truth to act upon those choices. I invite you to make this your constant way of being. Your spirit will become stronger and stronger by being fed daily with the infused nourishment of divine, spiritual energy with ideas ready to pour into you at the maximum amount needed every day.

As you learn to respond and practice in this way, your ability will grow until this is *always* your nature. Eventually, every thought will not just be from your mind, but from the oneness with your spirit's understanding and from Mine united with all of Divine's. Then great and mighty changes will take place, not only in your life but literally begin to turn the tide of your physical body from its downward spiral of deterioration and death.

Few people have been diligent in constantly living their lives with the enhancement of God's Light. Most have let the concerns of the world draw them away. They have prayers for several weeks and then they fade off. They come with a desire that begins to grow and then wanes as they are distracted. They come in prayer when the difficulties arise, then the prayers decline when life is a bit easier. Some people will study *about* God and His ways but do not come sufficiently in prayer and worship to be *with* God and receive the very Light necessary to put Love into the words and bring My gospel and Atonement into a living reality.

Most people in this world are filled with the patterns that distract and separate them from their true natures and spirit beings. Some of the world's fallen nature teachings appear to be good, but they are not filled with life and God's Light. Acting from the ideas of the world alone will continue to put distorted energy into the physical body which will continue in its deterioration. There is a difference between ideas filled with God's Truth and Love and those ideas received from just the world alone. Please ponder what I have just said here. All that you do can only be life-giving if done with Me and the Divine Father.

Chapter 3
Your True Divine Nature

Innately your divine nature is in your spirit. Fallen nature, however, weakens your spirit's capacity to bring forth this true nature. Without ample spiritual Light as nourishment, there is a lack of your true nature's power that is able to come through and be expressed in your life. Your spirit needs to become stronger. In order to create a stronger connection between your spirit and your physical being, I would that you put attention and awareness into strengthening your spirit to bring forth your true nature. This happens most powerfully through prayer. This alliance will illuminate your mind, your heart, and every cell of your body with divine power and capacity. This connection and interaction is part of what I offer to bring forth in you. Your spirit and divine nature's power and capacity are *so much more* than you currently are experiencing. So much more; so much more! Oh, please, dear one, realize how vitally important this strengthening of your spirit and true nature is. Come, feast on the Light and Love the Father and I have to give to you. Come. Come. Come.

As this holy union and divine guidance progress, you will not only know God's Will for your life but will also have the capacity to live it to the ultimate because My Gift can overcome the separation of your spirit from your body while in this Earth life. Most may think: *Oh, this is for the great prophets or someone who is much more righteous than I am. It is not for me!* Yes, it is for *you*!

I created your *own individual* Gift of your *perfection*, a spiritual formation of Light with all that you need to take you to the completion of your exaltation, moving forward every day. I have created such a glorious life for absolutely everyone! Very few *even begin* to believe the spiritual greatness that I have prepared for them! Oh, the greatness that can be in your life! This ultimate exaltation is the Gift I desire so deeply to give to *you*! Hear me, dear one. Pray right now so you can receive a testimony of this greatness of you! This is not pride. This is your true nature. I desire to restore you to the fullness of your glory. This restoring—bringing you forth to your greatness—glorifies the Father!

Take no thought as to how long it will take to rise up unto the fullness of your greatness of which I speak. There are years when you may think: *I do not know if I am moving forward at all.* Be diligent anyway. As you continue, I *promise* you the day will come when there will be a tipping point. A massive amount of change will take place in you; a great acceleration will lift your whole being, changing your physical nature. The fallen nature will fade away and will be replaced by the increase of your holy, true nature. This can continue, until there is a rapid momentum as you and I nurture the new you. Later, I will give much more detail to the various individual life paths that one could follow while ascending through the fullness of My Gift.

Meaningful Spiritual Experiences
In different ways, many people have had a profound, spiritual experience which stands out far above other spiritual experiences. In this great, significant moment they may have, for example, a sensation of Light filling their being, a joyful vibrating energy, or a 'burning in the bosom'. Truly, something different is going on, and they may conclude they have been Born Again. Several things could actually be taking place. One experience could be when the Holy Ghost is sending a strong *testimony*, a knowing beyond the mind, a witness to the heart of My gospel and that I am the Savior, the Redeeming One.

A second possibility, which can also attend the first, is a complete *conversion and commitment* to Me as their Savior—the beginning of turning one's life over to Me. The weeks or months that follow these experiences often seem enhanced, and righteous desires fill the thoughts with feelings of being empowered to live in a holier manner. As important as these moments are, they actually are not *the* Born Again experience I am speaking of. This first vital step, which can be compared to the 'conception' of life, needs time to develop and mature.

After your 'conception', continue to follow My guidance. There will be a multitude of lessons you will be led through to support you in recognizing and letting go of *all* negative patterns. Many of these are 'blind spots', the subtleties of deception that are part of the culture you live in and what has been taught generation after generation. Ask in sincere prayer to see where you have been blind and to hear what you have not heard before. I will move you through experience after experience to recognize and then gradually and steadily reduce the false understanding and false nature while increasing the true understanding and your true nature until you are ready for a complete conversion, ready to be 'born'. I will finalize the burning away of *all* your fallen nature and completely fill your being with Light and the new glory—*now* you are Born Again! Oh, how I rejoice for this glorious experience with you!

Born into Greater Glories

Now you are truly born anew, *never* to return to any of the old fallen nature, its patterns and ways or even to its influences. In this *first true* Born Again experience, your body is now in a newness of glory, even the first level of Light and Glory, which I call a Telestial Glory. With this degree of Light, there will be a greater expression of the Gifts of the Spirit. As a 'new being' you will learn and grow relatively quickly because it is a state of glory and not a fallen, deteriorating condition. In the beginning, like a baby or child, you will advance and increase through new levels of health, strength, and vitality. Now you are ready to begin the second phase, a greater part of My Gift.

Second Birth, Second Glory
Ultimately there are two more levels of glory. When you complete the first phase, you will again enter into a mighty change and be ready to have a *second* Born Again conversion into the next level of Light and Glory, which I call a Terrestrial Glory. In this glory, there will be an expansion of true miracles.

One possibility in this phase is to be changed into a translated state where the physical body is put into a state of *suspended life*. All beings upon this earth, who have been translated, such as the City of Enoch and Melchizedek's City of Salem, went through this second Born Again experience and were in a Terrestrial or Zion glory.

In this beautiful stage of your evolving, you will learn and practice utilizing new powers and abilities which will become your everyday capacity. This is the glory where even more will be restored to your physical being. This is a time for the refinement of your spiritual excellence.

Third Birth, Third Glory
I have prepared, even yet, the greatest of all glories for you, even a Celestial Glory, the infinite glory. There is a *third* Born Again experience where the body is made immortal with powers and capacities and, in time, developing the fullness of our great God. Such glory is not comprehensible in your current state; however, one day

you will know the exquisite felicity of such a hallowed and glorified life. I have already seen and experienced you in your holiest perfection.

In this glory, your physical body will advance to be created and formed as if it had been directly born of God. It is My cherished and holy blessing to be the One to transfer this Divinity to you. Again, I have already carefully and perfectly prepared all *specifically for you*! Even now, I hold you in My mind and heart in this glorified state which brings such sweet peace to My Soul.

Ascending of Great Beings for this Earth's Boost
What I am proclaiming is that this exalted Celestial state can be achieved in this life. *This is the fullness of My Gift!* You may ask, *Has this ever been done by someone on this earth before?* Yes, though rarely; Elijah was one. There have been others. I have carefully prepared strong ones for the Earth at this time to receive this highest glory. This assent is necessary to give the boost of greater energy and increased Divine Light to lift the world to a greater glory and create Zion for My return.

Please, please, please, hear My call to *you* to join the ranks of glorified beings to assist in this mighty victory! Cast out all thoughts that you are unworthy, that you can never achieve this exalted state, or that it is too far away. Put these judgments aside. Instead, draw forth your spirit's deepest desires to rise up in your full greatness! Your spirit is very worthy; your spirit is divine and holy. You *are* a child *of God*! Let this reality sink in and be a deeper influence upon you.

Truth Replacing the False
Everyone has many experiences which are not necessarily from their true self but come from decisions and actions out of various influences and false programming in the physical form. Yet, all experiences are valuable and, with Me, are for strengthening you to establish the true nature in your physical being. The false illusions and fallen nature patterns which temporarily exist in your body are unrighteous. If there is any portion of fallen nature within, your body will continue to deteriorate. The fallen nature is the true nature of Satan, the fallen one. Though currently, this invasive energy may exist in you, *it is not the true you*; it is not who *you* really are. Any feelings or thoughts of unworthiness are false illusions. Again, your experiences are not evidence of your true self; they are just experiences. The physical body's innate nature is to fulfill the 'full measure of its creation', to rise up to its most divine form.

We must bring in the greater Light so that the Light will consume the darkness until it is no more. Your body will change. Then your spirit will be able to live in perfect, total harmony with your body. Your divine true nature will be the full directing force with the influence, not just from the physical mind, but also from your spirit's heart and mind with the holiness and the godliness that you truly are. Again, if there is even the smallest negative thought that would say you are not worthy, proclaim in

My name a dismissal of that thought, then ask to receive the Light that holds your true nature. Though I greatly desire this for you, I cannot choose for you. *You* must be the one to *choose* this. Please, dear one, come and claim your true nature!

This is such a precious part of the Gift I have for you—to completely restore your divine, godly nature! Please, seek and receive this. I stand ready, eager, and desire greatly to complete My work with your spirit by delivering and infusing this divine, holy power into your physical body, even to be exalted and full of life. Come; be totally alive in Me. Let's dismiss the spirit of death and deterioration. Instead, My Light will be illuminating daily in you. Oh, what a glorious thought for Me! Oh, how I desire to give this Gift to you!

Be constant in this. Let not one day pass where you are pulled away by the busyness of the world from our precious Sacred Time together. Every day I have something new to impress upon you, something new to give to you—awareness, guidance, direction, holy Light, Love—filling you and nurturing you continually. When there is a negative thought, then use your power; call upon your spirit and Mine to come together. Work with Me saying: *Dear Christ, cast the energy of this thought out of me now and bring forth the truth of my being.* Pray for the understanding of the truth to replace the negative thought. Pray for Love to fill your being. Pray for your spirit to receive that great truth. Praise the Heavens and express gratitude that the door of Light to your being may be opened fully and even expand.

Frequently have sincere Sacred Time in the morning, in the evening, and throughout the day. Be constant that you have an outpouring that will build and strengthen you. Your spirit needs daily, constant nutrition to be strengthened and guided back into purity, away from the false and fallen nature. This body is to be fully reclaimed by you because you are God-kind. This clearing and claiming is to be complete until *only* Light and Truth exist in your being. Again, I ask you to receive the fullness of this precious Gift that I have for you. Any portion of the fallen nature is *never really* you, for it is the nature of the fallen one. Do not let his nature stay in your body.

By My name and with My power and Me at your side infusing Truth and Love into you, come to know who you *really* are. If you study yourself by looking at the patterns of the fallen ways and the opinions of this world, you will *not* get to know yourself, not the way I want you to know yourself. Your spirit is your true you. It is the purer part of you that I aspire for you to appreciate and know so that I may completely unite your spirit and body. Be open to this unification. Prepare to receive My Light and Love to be alive, wholly alive in Me, so your spirit will be able to completely fuse with your body, never to separate.

The day is coming for Me to be here on this earth. There will then be different circumstances and different conditions. Fallen nature will not exist on this planet, only the exalting ways will. We are now to dismiss this fallen nature in your beings by inviting in the true nature, yea, even My Gift to you, the full living Gift I have to give to you—your fully alive being. Then this new nature, the true nature, will also be in this physical world. In the world to come, all will not only confess My name but also fully receive the Atonement and come to be one with Me.

Future New World
Those who will remain here upon the earth as I come to take up My holy new position will be in a new world. Since it will not have any of the fallen nature, it will not have death from disease or deterioration from old age. There will be those who transition. They will leave this planet, but they will not go through death as you know it. Many will have their physical bodies illuminated to such a degree that they may move as the angels move and may visit or be in other realms and dimensions. Many will stay here on Earth the entire time as I continue to prepare this earth to one day become the highest of Glories and Light.

The time is now! The time is *right now*, beginning from the very minute you read this message. Be diligent in daily time with Me and your Heavenly Parents. Be passionate about this. Be devoted. Keep asking to hear anew, to hear true, to hear pure. With Me and in My Name cast out anything that would keep you from moving forward—every false thought, anything that would say you are less than pure, divine, and holy, or that you are not connected to the Heavens, for you are—in your true self you are! Our Love constantly pours into you. Recognize it. Receive it. Open the door that you might let more of this Love in!

I am the Deliverer of this pure Love. I have prepared your exaltation. Receive My Gift and be alive in Me, fully alive. This aliveness is different from being alive as you are now—this alive is eternally alive! Your spirit is already eternally alive, and I am sustaining it. Desire for your whole being to be alive—alive in Me! Be fed daily until the impressions are clear and strong, and thoughts in your mind are from your spirit and combined with Divine's. Align with the Heavens and your physical body will be empowered, your emotions *always* with peace, joy, exhilaration, gratitude, harmony, and love at *all* times. These ways are to be your constant feelings, your constant way of being in this physical body, this precious physical body that you have been given, to illuminate with Me, to be just like the Father's.

Begin Now

Let us begin now. Make your goal greater than you have ever done before. *Do not dilute anything.* Make all I have spoken your absolute commitment *now*. Please, I am asking you to come in prayer, in My name, through My nature, and through the Holy channel and the Gift that I have prepared for you. Call upon the Holy Father and receive the *increase* of Light I will then give to you through the Holy Gift of the Atonement prepared so carefully just for you. *Begin now, My precious one; begin now!*

Alive in Christ – *The Gift*

Chapter 4
Experience Divine Nature

Deep in My heart, I have such a peace and reverence for you. Yet there is a barrier in you that keeps you from My love and the very Gift I have prepared for you to receive. You do not yet understand who you are, how glorious you are, and how much I do love you. Let's explore together factors that can remove this barrier and open you to My love for you.

Sacred Prayer Time

Prayer and our Sacred Time together is the vital foundation. Through all generations of time people have been taught to pray to God. It has been taught, practiced, and performed in many different ways and styles. God accepts them all. Prayer has been emphasized in many messages sent forth already in My name and in your behalf. Biblical record tells of some of My teachings and gives a brief example of one of My prayers. *Come, learn what sincere and effective mighty prayer is.*

I am asking you now to increase and deepen our prayer time together. I desire for you to realize how important prayer is in order for the impressions of the Holy Ghost and My Spirit to stimulate your mind, expand your understanding, and stir your spirit. Through our Sacred Time of communication in prayer, it will awaken your heart as well as strengthen your overall being to fulfill My desires for you. I cannot emphasis this enough.

Move forward in prayer and sacred communication. Move forward to become fully alive, which aliveness comes by our association, yours and Mine. When you are in sincere prayer calling upon the Holy Father, you are more open to Me and Heaven's powers. Your sincerity opens your being to receive greater amounts of Light and Love that I will pour into you. *Prayer is the power to realize, understand, and obtain Life through Me.*

Prayers are usually offered in small doses, yet this is something that needs to be the greatest focus in your entire life. I understand that the world and others make many demands and claims upon you and your time. One of the ways is the many hours you often must work in order to just sustain your basic living needs. I understand that. I also recognize you may have taken on more than one job and may also be pursuing further education or are very involved with other good and important causes. I am asking you to deeply consider that there is another way, even though you may *think* there is not. If you are in a situation in which the demands of life don't leave adequate time for prayer and enough sleep, pray fervently for a way to have that quiet time necessary to do this vital, holy work with Me.

Chapter 4 –Experience Divine Nature

I yearn for you to have the time to be with Me. When your desire is 100% pure—every part of you longing for it—I will open up a way so that you do have that time. Often when free discretionary time occurs, it is filled with other activities that are of less value. In order to receive that which is freely offered from Me, you must be completely open and receptive. Prayer takes time. If you are not in daily, adequate Sacred Time, you are not making yourself as open and receptive as needed to receive the *Gift* I have for you. Let's make this change.

I am calling you. Come. Please know I am grateful for any moments you do spend in prayer. If you have not prayed for an hour or more daily then even twenty minutes may seem a long time for you. If that is the situation you are in, I am giving you a new standard to have an hour of prayer—at least. Now you might already be spending an hour or two or even more every day in prayer—wonderful! This extended amount of time may be beyond that which you have ever experienced before; however, you will grow into this. You will learn to comfortably pray for a longer period of time. It will be a beautiful time when you and I are together with the Father.

You may have little children, and this may cause a great challenge also. The call of parenthood, especially motherhood, is a 24 hour-a-day job, and I understand that, too. In the same manner, you also are to look intently with all your heart, might, mind, and soul to find a way for the time to open up for you even with those conditions. Ask and pray for that, and I will help you find the way. Again, *when it is presented to you, recognize and take the hour to have our sacred, personal prayer time.*

Making These Truths Your Nature

As you continue to read, you will learn some beautiful ideas and principles, some things that you have not considered before. All of these ideas can only take place with full effect in your life when we, together, have our sweet hour of prayer. Even though I speak with all My heart, and you are completely open to receive the spirit of My thoughts, yet do not nurture our relationship through prayer and Sacred Time, these words cannot take life in you. These words must be *more* than just heard in the mind and witnessed in the heart; they must be *developed in the soul.*

The mind is not the director of your salvation. Your spirit and your spirit's Love is the greater power in you. My Spirit and your spirit working together will give you the power needed to transform your physical body and to make all the changes in you to be of divine nature.

Now, even though these thoughts and teachings can be rather sobering, it is not meant to be heavy. How can you be absolutely dedicated and 100% committed without feeling rigidity, worry, stress, discouraged, or even depressed? The seriousness of the world often has pressure with it, and its teachings can be very demanding. Underneath that heaviness is a false belief this great transformation I speak of cannot really take place. Let's dismiss that. My message, My Gift is to lift the soul and lighten the heart. My yoke is easy when I walk along beside you while we lovingly work together.

The Part the Mind Plays
The mind will have a tendency to say: *I must study more, work harder, and be in control and more disciplined.* It is not under the control of the mind that brings salvation, though, yes, the mind must understand. Because of subtle, incorrect definitions and false generational teachings, you must receive in a new way. Your whole spirit must be fed by our association in which My Love and Light pour into you through your spirit and then into every particle of your physical being. *Then* your mind can be illuminated to understand further beyond its own reasoning. I delight in My edifying you in this higher way.

Knowing yourself is not sufficiently taught in the scriptures, although there is some mention of it. This knowledge is so vitally important. Why? Because the identity given to you in the world was designed out of the opinions of others, the false traditions, generational patterns, and your own desire to prove your worth by your works. In reality, *your good works come out of the divine worth you already are.*

A misunderstanding has also been taught that you are an enemy to God. *Fallen nature* which is in the physical body is the enemy to God, but your spirit, your true nature, is *not* an enemy. Your true identity is a beautiful, holy child who is from the nature of God.

So, you come with criticism towards yourself because you do not really know yourself. You know the fallen nature that has been in your physical body that you are dealing with. It is those patterns and ways that you sometimes get upset with, the things you are trying to overcome. Yes, I would have you overcome those ways, but *first begin* with feeding, nurturing, empowering, and strengthening the part of you that is pure, the part of you that is divine.

That awakened life and vitality of your spirit comes because of our association and our private, personal time together. When you pray and open up, I am there. I am the One that stands between you and the Father. You pray unto the Father, but you are also working with Me. It is My intent to take you to the Father, and so I will first fill you with the very Light that is necessary to make the transition.

Faith in Communication
Usually people begin with all the 'instructions' or commandments, a list of all the things they need to do and the changes they need to make. But I say to you, begin by holy communication, a sincere desire to come and be open and receive. In some ways, you go to the specifics: *These are all the things I would like to have changed in me, dear God.* Before we make the changes, we need to gather the very Light 'substance' that is going to form the new patterns in your physical body so that these changes can take place.

Chapter 4 – Experience Divine Nature

In a prayer of gratitude, express your love for God. When you are in such prayer, the spirit of the Eternal Mother and Father—Their beautiful, Holy Essence—is with you; Their Light, Their Eternal Truth, and Their Love radiate from Them to you. I also hold Their Spirit within Me to deliver this Holy Essence which is also in and around these words. We are talking about energy, an infinite God energy. It is a whole sphere of beautiful essence, a Light that distills upon your being and enters into you. *This is the beginning and the origin of all that you are and can ever desire to create.* This is what gives life and makes you be fully alive!

Let Me give you another analogy so that you can better understand. Let's say that somebody is ill, and the body is limp and perhaps even unconscious. So you say to this weak, unconscious person: *You have to do all these things. You have to do this and this and this and this.* Yet the body cannot do all those things; it cannot even move.

In some ways, you want yourself—your outward self, your physical self—to do all these things, to be all these things, to live all the commandments, and to take all those beautiful principles and virtues you'd like to have in your life and fulfill your highest expectations. You want your body to do that, but in order to do these Godly eternal ways and be this Godly eternal being in this physical body, there must first be the awakening, a greater consciousness from Spirit and Divine Light. There needs to be a healing to overcome the weaknesses which keep you from living to the greatest potential you so desire.

The Awakening

The body first must come out of its unconscious state. You may think that you are very conscious, but *compared* to the power of your spiritual knowing and the fullness of the Truth, you are not fully conscious, not the way I mean for you to be. You do not know in your conscious, physical mind what your spirit knows. You are veiled from your spirit's complete knowing, which is the *first veil,* separating you from the full power of your spirit. Though this awareness is still there, it is in a quieter state. This knowing in your spirit is from God, the Source of Eternal Truth, and is filled with power. We are to connect and open that divinity in you.

There is also a *second veil* or covering upon you that came from the *dark one*. It is a heavy, dulling reversal of all that is righteous. It is a dark, insidious death-causing energy. That is what is keeping you from your full life and vitality, causing your spirit to be unable to completely interface with your body. Many decisions are made from the patterns in the physical body influenced by this dark veil, the fallen nature. This nature is passed down from generation to generation and sustained by the experiences that you have had in this world where everything is distorted, turned around, and upside down. This must be removed. *This is My work; this is what My Atonement is for.* This is what I *so* desire to do with you.

Before you can be and do all your heart desires in righteousness, we must first awaken this dynamic part of you that is filled with Light and vitality. For this you need the *divine food* from the Eternal Mother and Father I so desire to serve to you. People are usually busy using their minds alone to monitor, control, and figure out how to make the desired improvements. The mind does not have that power to overcome all weaknesses; this simply cannot be done by the mind alone, not to the degree of excellence possible. Even the most disciplined people fall short. Your spirit being has a constant inflow of Light which then interfaces with your physical being—your thoughts, your emotions, and the physical body. What you need is an *abundance* of divine power which starts from the Origin of Life, the Glory from the Eternal Mother and Father, to flow into your being. This needs to not only be copious but also be a constant flow and increase, influencing your physical being as We intended.

Begin with the spirit of divinity and true nature to create, decide, act, and produce in the most powerful way. Your true essence will strengthen your power to create and bring to pass all righteous desires. Become alive with Me, fully alive, your spirit vitally alive in your being, *then* your power, capacity, strength, and knowing will be far greater. Instead of beginning with the physical capacities and the mind's ability, start from the origin of your holy heritage from God and let Me be your connection, your Mediator, and Teacher.

The Thinking and the Doing

You are to actively engage in many good works. However, to gain this greater life of which I am speaking, do not start with the physical capacity. Many people try to monitor their lives through activities alone. Instead, start with the greater divine nature already in you, the power of who you are. Let this divine power be added upon, multiplied, increased, and expanded. Though your spirit is in your body, it is not yet completely one with the body. Your spirit cannot be one with the physical form while it holds any of the distorted patterns and misunderstandings. Again, this is why I am here to transform your physical nature from its current state into an exalted state, step by step. Not only are we to lift the physical body to a higher level but also to transform the thinking process to fulfill its true purpose.

The mind is not the origin of creation; *God is.* True, you are to ponder all things. Your thinking is a vital part of your life's accomplishments and the door to open to move you forward. Your mind needs to be illuminated. This is why I have asked you to be prayerful and open with a sincere desire, asking for this glorious Light I give to illuminate, strengthen, and empower your spirit being. Then there will be a stirring within you. A change taking place in the physical body from that divine part of you, giving you the ability in this physical being of yours to righteously make the changes, do the things that you want to do, feel what you want to feel, and think the thoughts you want to think.

Power of Spirit in Words
You have had marvelous experiences before, even spiritual experiences, yet when you begin to describe them to someone else, the words cannot really completely

transfer to the other person what you have experienced. Words are beautiful conveyors. Oft times they give a beautiful *beginning* of understanding, but it is never quite like the experience itself. It just is not.

Even for you who have had the experience, it is not the same as the actual moment. When you try to relive it from your memory, you cannot experience the same *emotional impact* again as it was in the moment. Yet the experience had an impact upon you. It added to your life and became a part of you at the moment you *experienced* it.

You could also read wonderful ideas all day but there needs to be an awakening of a greater discovery deeper than conscious thought. These words I give you, though they are lovely and true, must not just be ideas transferred to your mind. As you read these words, they are going into your conscious mind, but I am also sending them to your spirit.

For these words to become more than just information, ask My Light and Spirit to open up the power of these words. Take time to peacefully come and be with Me. Yes, you will be using your words and your mind for this prayer, but you are going to find the more you step into the spirituality of our connection and receive My Light, the more you will experience My message to influence and feed your whole being. Your prayers, in time, will move into less conversation with words because you are noticing and experiencing the wholeness of what is taking place—Light is influencing your being.

This section would be a good place to **stop reading and have a prayer.** Ask to receive testimony of what I have been talking about. Ask for a stirring of increased desire to have a personal change in your life because of My words. Ask for My Light to fill you and prepare your being in the manner I have been relaying through these words. Let what I have presented already become alive in you. Ask that your spirit be fed to *experience* Truth and Light. Please, come in prayer now. *Experience* what I am speaking about.

Chapter 5
Spirit Gives You Life

Let's talk more about what I mean by *experiencing* My messages. What is that like? One way you may receive My Light is by getting an impression, a new thought or awareness in your mind. As you allow more time for My Light to fill you, you can notice a feeling, a movement of Divine energy in your physical body. This Light is influencing your physical structure, balancing emotions, and illuminating thoughts and understandings. This will build in time and can make a *permanent, significant change* in you. This is what we want. *This is our goal.*

Your spiritual awakening is not something that can be fully conveyed to another person. Transference cannot be given to another by words alone. When all are filled with the Spirit, however, everyone can be edified, not only from the words but also because the Light of God is present. It is Spirit; it is Light that does the transferring. It is Spirit; it is Light that gives you Life.

Experience Your Spirit Self
I can tell you a lot about you. If I were to literally sit down with you, I could tell you about your personality,

your thoughts, your beliefs, your feelings, and your nature. I could give you the name of who you were before you came here, but all this would not be the same as experiencing yourself. There will be days, if you have not already experienced this before, when you will simply have a deeper connection to who you are. This is beyond words. *To deeply experience the wonder of your spirit self is a separate form of peace all of its own.*

To go out into this world and interface, doing all the marvelous things you would like to do to your maximum capacity, you really need to know who you are. I do not mean to know *about* you; I mean that you *experience* your spirit and your true nature. You will feel yourself, feel your divinity. I tell you that your spirit being is different than your physical being, though there are some similarities. Yet the two will come together, be unified and be one. I promise I will completely restore your true nature as you continue with prayer and Sacred Time with Me.

All the great ways of your physical life will be added upon, expanding your goodness and the wonderful being you are. Your physical being must be raised to the higher standard and to the beautiful ways that your spirit being already is. Your spirit being will not step down to the lower ways that have been in your life in this fallen world. The only way anyone can come to experience Truth is by *feeling and understanding* it with an illumination beyond what is usually known, that which comes from God and My Gift to you.

You will be able to know yourself, to be introduced to that self, and that self can then interface more with your physical being. Then, when you experience your spirit in your physical being, you will be able to move forward greatly empowered. If you have ever felt some sort of spiritual high, you may have thought: *Oh, if life could be this way all the time!* It can when there is the constant nourishment from Divine Light through your spirit.

Restoring Divine Peace

Often you become calm and peaceful when circumstances around you seem to be flowing smoothly and events are going well. My Peace is different. The Peace I bring comes from Divinity—a peace which is part of the Nature of the Holy Love of God. It is far beyond any peace of this world. Your spirit holds this Peace, and you can only experience it with Divine Spirit Light. I desire to not only open you to the Peace you have in your spirit but to even greater Peace, the Divine Nature of God and Their Peace which is an eternal, unconditional Peace.

This is why I again mention daily Sacred Time with Me. You are going to need **one to two hours** or sometimes more every day because you are asking for the fullness of the Gift I want to openly give to you. Let this openness be open on both sides, you to Me and Me to you. I am open to give; you must be open to Me and receive.

Yes, I am with you constantly in the busyness of other activities, but We must have our quiet Sacred Time together. As you go to bed at night, your body becomes quiet. That hour before you go to bed would be a beautiful time for us to have a discussion about the day for you to feel My Light come into your being that there might be a settling of the day. Let's go back through the day and clear out anything that was disturbing—reliving any moments again to your greatest desire and giving enlightenment to any portion of the day. *It is possible to spiritually review and then redo the day as if it had been ideal.*

This quiet, peaceful time in prayer is a good time to receive new insight. Ask for greater inspiration in a situation you did not know what to do or how to handle it. Even if at the moment you still do not know a greater way to handle a situation, I will fill you with the Light to begin the change in your being. *All your activities and emotions will be recreated as if you had lived each moment in righteousness.* Divine Essence will bring to you the insight needed and the better way to handle your life. Then you may go to bed in peace and the Spirit of God's Love will continue to bless you during your sleep, preparing you to be ready and spiritually fed for the next day.

Becoming One with Us
I want and need this time with you. I want you to talk openly to Me and the Father, for We are of Oneness. When you talk to Him, you talk to Me; when you talk to Me, you talk to Him. There is no difference whether you speak to the Father or to Me, yet I am the Christ, and, at this point, I am between you and God, the Father, and I

am preparing to give the fullness of all that I have received from the Father and take you to Him. His fullness is in Me, or in other words, all of His Nature is in Me. This is how I am in the Father and the Father is in Me. My ultimate Gift is to deliver *His full Glory to you,* even as it is in Me.

I must have the time because what I have to give to you must be delivered in the wholeness of your open, sincere desire to be with Us. Discover your soul's desire to be with Us, to communicate and discuss everything about life you can possibly discuss and to allow Our Presence to be *felt*. You will find your body's ability to interface with Our Glory will be immensely enhanced and magnified. It is something that I can talk about but to *experience* it is very different. Let's make this happen.

You may say: *I have no idea what being in Your Presence and interfacing with Your Glory is like. I do not know how.* That is alright. You do not need to know how beforehand; you simply need to affirm: *I am here and willing.* After a while, you will have a clear idea of what it is like because you will have felt and experienced Our Glory and Presence. Again, people want to 'figure it out' as if the description or information and the 'right words' to say are all that is needed. You must come to have Our Divine Love and Light in increase, moving through your spirit being to awaken you to the Truth of your divinity. You *are* glorious, absolutely *glorious*!

Truth is a *living* entity, a substance of Light and power. When this living truth within you becomes so active that it will empower the holy patterns in your physical body as it was designed to do. You will find yourself naturally acting ideally in every moment. You will be so vibrant with Our Truth and Love that you will have all you need in your life. Really? *Really*!

The reason I am telling you this is because most people want and strive to have mastery of life but don't *really* believe such a way of living is possible. I am raising your sights of possibility and offering hope. I am telling you it is possible—for *you*! With the constant increase and peak of Our Light in you, this is a reality. I am asking you to have faith in such and bring this excellence into your life.

I want you to be taught everything there is from the holiness of God. Our Father knows *everything* about you—your inner thoughts and emotions and even how and why you will respond in every situation. He is intricately aware of every tiny aspect of you and your life. When in adequate Sacred Time, the Holy Divine Essence that comes into your spirit being will have an influence upon you physically. Then throughout the day, you will be illuminated with thoughts, feelings, emotions, direction, empowerment, strength, balance, intelligence, and wholeness in all of your being.

In whatever you are doing, your words will become powerful. They will not just be words of vibration and sound but filled with the divinity and power. Words are like containers that can hold the powerful essence of what they are to convey. As your personal Light brightens, your words become powerful and fruitful. Your influence will be mighty. Oh, the *powerful* work we can do together. What a wonderful life to live!

Holy Order of Things
There is a holy order in creation which begins with God's Love. Holy Divine Essence is inseparable from Eternal Truth and unconditional Love. Our Eternal Parents are the Origin of Creation; out of Their Eternal Essence comes all else.

The world has taught the reverse. The world has said: *The mind is the origin of creation. Get information. Knowledge is everything.* Mankind takes glory to himself and is puffed up in the pride of intelligence and the power of the brain. I tell you reading and studying any and all information will have a much more profound result with the influence of *sincere prayer and acknowledging the Source of all Truth.* People believe society is advancing very quickly, but compared to what could be, it is slow and dull. Each and every person's ability to learn would be dramatically greater, and the world's progression would be infinitely further along than where it is even at this time—simply by adding real prayer.

Those who acknowledge God say: *Read and study the scriptures.* I say it is good to read the scriptures—when you always read them with divine prayer. *Then* the scriptures will have a deeper impact and fulfill their purpose, illuminating and feeding your spirit. Please, do not read scriptures just to become knowledgeable. Only with prayer will you understand and *receive the power* these words can release. The true meaning and spirit of the scriptures will be greater than ever before and in a manner that cannot be conveyed by sound or words alone. I stand ready to release this profound power and Light. I am the Word and will give life to all Truth, written and spoken.

I ask you to *really* come and have a relationship with Me; know Me personally. I so desire this! Let's have conversation; talk openly and then *notice* My response. Seek with *all* of your heart and soul to find our time to be together. Ask Me to work with you on that, and I will assist you in making this time.

Remember My Gift is freely offered without restraint on My part, though you must open up and do your part too. The delivery will be in a holy order according to My wisdom. At first, I will simply illuminate you with Light and Love which will gently make a transformation in your thoughts, your emotions, and your physical body's health and well-being. The flow of My constant Light will increase. You will also grow in recognizing and sensing My Light and Love as an inspiration and transformation in you.

I would like you to be Alive in Me, for the fullness of the Father's Eternal Life is in Me, and I desire to fill you with

Our Love. I am pure Love, and God, the Father, is pure Love; you are also pure Love in your true nature which must be nurtured with Our Love. Your love will grow, and your true nature will be strengthened to experience, know, and cherish who you really are. Then your eternal nature will have the capacity to influence your physical being, illuminating all aspects of your life. Oh, how I look forward to the greater joy you will have to live and be your true self, your greatest self, your divine self!

Walk Forward in Prayer
Your life will take on an empowering, whole *newness* with this greater, sacred prayer I speak of. The heaviness in life comes from fallen nature, and fallen nature responses to the world around you. There is not heaviness upon life *at all* when you are one with Me. The Light, the joy, the peace, the uplift, the hope, the encouragement, the faith all come when you are filled and fed and nurtured amply. It comes from Me daily, every moment by the Divinity from the Eternal Father and the Mother. I come to deliver all to you. Be alive. Oh, so *alive*! Words alone will not describe; words *cannot* describe that joy!

Pray about the words of this chapter you have already read. Ask to receive and feel the whole essence of My words. Ask for all My words to become one with you. Do so with sincerity. Learn how to expand your ability to pray so that you are more comfortable and eagerly look forward to spending ample time with Me and the Father. Our communication is something that can always keep improving. Come to know the Father as well as I do. **Stop**

right now and let's have some sacred prayer time. Let this be a delight to you!

Constant Peace, Joy, and Hope
Let the experiences of beautiful, spiritual, and peaceful memories be ongoing, continual experiences. That is the goal you and I are working for. Let's create being *vitally* alive every day with love, joy, and peace your *constant* emotions and wisdom your constant companion. This is personally offered to you—in this physical world—before I come again. *My invitation is to receive the fullness of what I have to give to you.*

I know I have said this many times before, but the pattern is so set as to let the words stop with the mind. After a while, the mind will become annoyed with the repeats and say, *Alright already! Let's do something about this!*

This is the beginning of your next level of becoming one with your spirit and Me. In this together we will create Zion. One day we will raise this world to a Celestial, Heavenly Glory, likened to the very home where God, our Eternal Father and Mother dwell. This is where we are going. Come with Me.

Chapter 6
Life Path, Life Plan

My dear one, please know all has been carefully planned for this most unique life on Earth, and it is an important part of your eternal progression. Our glorious Father in Heaven, in His perfection, has thoroughly prepared a way for you to transition through life. He is *literally* the Father of your spirit being; you are of Him.

Being Away for Learning
You have been learning, developing, and advancing for eons of time—*imagine that*! At times you have dwelt in the Heavens, our glorious home. There are also times when you have 'gone away to school' to learn outside of the stronger influence from our Eternal Parents' Glory. In these times away everyone is placed into a state of amnesia, a 'veiled' state. Your personal internal Light, which is sustained to guide and direct you, still quietly holds the memory of what you have previously learned. My Light, which is identified as the *Light of Christ,* will always keep this inner Light in each person protected and sustained. All can increase the ability to access that Light and have this be an influence for decisions.

Through the different stages of our existence, there are a variety of these away-from-home times. At each juncture we meet with God, Our Father, to prepare for the next section of our personal life. This Earth life is one of those veiled times. You participated in the choices of your life plan with the Father's wisdom and guidance. An intention was set for particular lessons to be learned in certain conditions for your most ideal well-rounded education.

No one was sent here with a *plan to make mistakes*, develop a weakness, or commit a sin. All were given a physical body with certain conditions and weakness with the *plan to overcome* them. For example, one was not sent with a life plan to be an alcoholic or an abuser, though they may have been placed into an environment with that example and with a body that had ancestral patterns of these tendencies. It is given to *everyone* to choose to transform weaknesses into strengths, to resist temptations, and surmount sin. Again, this is where you and I are to work together—your desire and choice with My greater Light and Power.

Opposing Forces
God has placed you into this beautiful world with the Divine Light which offers life-giving, advancing influences and powers in the Earth to support and bless you. However, there are also *opposing* forces constantly working against you. You are dealing in a world in which the energies are quite imbalanced, distorted, and of the fallen nature, which is a deteriorating pattern where everything is set to decline in a state of depreciation. These same two great forces are working in you. I am here to

restore you to your true divine nature, to create a 'beautiful world' within you. *My intent is for you and I to then take this new way out into the world.*

One of the ploys of Satan is the lie that you are not *worthy*. People have even used the Scripture's warnings and the commandments as measuring sticks to judge themselves and others as undeserving. I am not discrediting the scripture's teachings, for I am the very one to support you in achieving these standards; however, it cannot be done by intently studying and memorizing the scriptures, learning the steps, and using only your own efforts and abilities. You are dealing with the opposing energies of the fallen one, which exist in your physical body. Many are struggling in their efforts to move out of this nature by their own merits alone and do not yet fully understand the part that is missing.

The subtle lies that you think, feel, and believe about yourself keep you from the very Gift that I do freely offer. What does the word *freely* mean? In the world, it means there is *no cost*; however, I have paid a great price. With My Gift, it means 'openly given with requirements'.

Does that mean that you have to be perfect before you can receive the redeeming grace? No, not at all! *You need My Redeeming Grace in order to be made perfect.* All I ask from you is your sincerity of heart and patience because I do not advance you without your awareness. With each step you must consciously choose with all of your being as you move forward. You must say: *Yes! This is what I want to have in my life.* And you must fully understand what that *'yes'* entails.

The moment I say this, many will immediately respond: *But I do want this. I want to be this beautiful way. I want to live all the wonderful principles and commandments I have been taught. I am doing everything I can, but I still struggle. I still have negative emotions. I still feel inadequate.* These feelings are the indications that you are still in the entrapment of fallen nature. You do not understand what is interfering and keeping you captive.

There is a distorted belief and misunderstanding that you must somehow 'save yourself' from your problems, weaknesses, or sins before you can really come to God. Perhaps you do come in prayer, but then, once receiving some enlightenment, you then decide to 'take it from there' and proceed forward to 'work it out' by yourself. Some also take another approach and wait for Me to bring their redemption and do not think they have any part except to wait. However, I say *first* come to Me in sincerity and *stay with Me* to resolve the false patterns that have been passed down for generations and are deeply embedded in your body. *Together* we can remove all barriers.

Working with Christ and His Redeeming Power
The way you *begin* to receive My Gift is with a complete, 100% decision to move forward *with Me*. You personally cannot *create* the redeeming power; your part is to choose to *receive* the power to overcome. Remember,

Chapter 6 – Life Path, Life Plan

'The power is Mine, the choice is thine.' Your decision must also be a complete and unified decision within your being. There can easily be conflicting desires and choices within you that you do not even realize. Ask Me to show you the contradicting beliefs you are blind to. I am here to help you see deeply within yourself, to remove any division in your decisions, and to establish complete congruity in your will.

We desire to fill you with the Divine Light *as you learn how to be in holy stewardship over the powers of God.* I would not hand you the keys to the car if you did not have a certain level of proficiency in handling the car, driving in traffic, and maintaining a vehicle. In like manner, I will not hand you Godly powers without teaching you how to thoroughly understand, practice, and use those powers. So, My portion is given to you freely, *without restraints* but yet *with requirements* to understand what you are being given. I also desire deeply, just as you do, for you to live the clearer and purer way of being. We are willing to give you the instructions, the power, and the ability to move forward as you learn to 'drive the car.'

Managing this physical body is definitely a major task and is much more than just understanding things mentally. Your physical being is intricately woven with responses and patterns from the teachings of mankind as well as the false traditions passed down through the generations. These are anchored in with automatic emotional responses that cause mindless reactions, habits and behaviors. I am here to help you open your whole being to Love and Truth in its pure form and to unify you with eternal ways.

There are also false traditions and teachings that have been inherited and are very subtle. Likewise, distorted definitions and altered meanings of words have created deceptions. These misleading teachings may seem true and good, but actually, they are not. For example, self-confidence is highly rated and is sought after as a virtue. However, I say there is a definite difference between self-confidence, which can support pride, and knowing and experiencing one's true, infinite worth in the eyes of God. One important part of My Atonement is to shine Light upon these false teachings; then together, you and I can apply My power and Light to change these patterns and overcome weaknesses.

Life Plans and Resurrection
All God's children have a personal life plan wisely designed by our Heavenly Father which they agreed to and joyfully accepted. This plan was designed with variables which support the same outcome of learning and development. Each plan has been prepared to perfectly support and guide each person's optimum growth. However, because of individual agency, everyone is free to make any choice whatsoever which, of course, will bring a different outcome. Because of the Atonement and the grace of God, regardless of choice, all experiences are for each person's refinement and will bring forth one's ultimate learning. Oh, my precious child, I greatly desire for you

Chapter 6 – Life Path, Life Plan

to know and live the beautiful life plan Father prepared for you. We are ready to support you in this glorious plan.

As you basically understand, all people born into this world have inherited fallen nature which brings a downward deterioration and a death-directed pattern to the body. All of this distorted and declining nature is *conquerable* and even death is only temporary. A *variety* of ways to overcome death and enter into living eternally with one's spiritual and physical body united have been created by My Atonement. This assures and confirms that everyone's spirit and divine nature is safe and protected by Me. I would like to discuss with you different options of moving into eternal life.

Physical Death, Life Review, and Resurrection
The most *common* way is to go through a physical death and then be resurrected. When a person dies, the spirit goes to a realm for a *life review* to carefully prepare for this great advancement of resurrection. Everyone is given opportunity to recognize and release the lies and false ways and to accept and lovingly embrace eternal truth. When each precious spirit is complete and ready, together we joyfully restore life to the physical body. The Heavens celebrate as that being re-enters and victoriously takes up the body. Let's take a closer look at this process.

The purpose of this after-death *life review* is a time to choose *anew* and spiritually recreate one's life. The amount of time this reconstruction takes depends on the individual's overall eternal advancement, and the conditions from their earth life. *Everyone still deals with the emotions and thought processes they had while on Earth.* To gain the greatest learning it is necessary to carefully review one's life with expanded understanding and added different perspectives. This review is very thorough; when complete, a spirit being is then ready for resurrection.

Though all people participate in their own resurrection, the degree of participation varies greatly for each person and ranges from 1% up to 99% . This depends on each person's personal development and advancement. All are required, however, to put forth their all. I then pour through them the additional wisdom, ability, and power to complete the resurrection. This involvement for every person is a significant part in the overall learning and advancement as a God-kind.

Other Death Phenomenon
Let Me share a portion more about the situation with individuals who have had a *near death experience*. Their return does not achieve the established resurrection requirements. The reason for their return is because their life plan was not complete, and it was wisdom in Me that they return. In these circumstances, I have given authority to a person *in Heaven* to proclaim and establish the reuniting of the spirit and body. Upon return these individuals may not remember anything, or they may remember a portion or the entire sojourn. With their tran-

sition through the veil and back they are generally stronger in their resolve to live closer to their life plan. They will eventually be a candidate for a normal death and the resurrection experience.

I would also like to address another rare and unusual experience that is part of the death phenomenon and that is being *raised from the dead state*. This transition also does not fulfill the resurrection requirements, and that person will most likely still go through another death, have a *life review* and a traditional resurrection. Like those with the near death experience, some have memory of their time on *the other side* while others do not, but again, there is a continual influence which supports that person to stay true to course for the remainder of their Earth life. In all such cases there was the involvement of someone *on Earth* with the faith, gift, and power to restore life. Because I am the One to overcome all death and hold the keys to eternal life, this cannot be done without My permission and authority.

Quickened Resurrection
Another possibility in advancing into eternal life with the physical body is overcoming death by experiencing an *immediate or quickened resurrection.* In this the spirit being and I together lift up the body soon after death. Those individuals who are well advanced in the mastery of Light and life do not need time for a life review after death because with them I have already opened up the same understanding and expansion of awareness that one would accomplish after death.

This quickened resurrection can take place in as little as twelve minutes or up to three days after the departure from the body. The spirit will spend that time gathering further instruction, preparing for the mission to follow, or ministering to others such as I did. Then once in the resurrected body, one may either move to a new sphere, a different realm and dimension, or may remain here upon Earth. This quickened resurrection will be much more prevalent during Zion—the Millennial Reign that is soon to come.

For you to gain the greatest learning from this Earth experience, ongoing reviews with Me are necessary. I will add different perspectives and enlarged understanding to the overall situation. The review of an experience and the exalting of one's choices can be done thoroughly and on a current basis by spiritually working with Me. Having timely reviews with Me will offer new insights, add refinement, and expanded perfection for each moment. *This makes it much easier to stay close to your optimum life plan Father created for you.*

You can begin right now and take much sacred time to delve deeply into your own life and see it through My eyes. The greatest way is to be so continually connected with Me that My added Light and divine awareness are with you at all times. Again, I offer to you My Atonement for daily moment-to-moment application as My enduring blessing.

Chapter 7
Eternalness While On Earth

Eternalness of life is when a person's body is so completely filled with glorious Light and life that it does not experience death at all. Even with the physical body being in a state of *eternalness,* there are a variety of different possibilities. One possibility is to be **translated** in which the body's mortal state and death are put into a *suspension*. A translated being may remain on Earth for a specific time and for a particular purpose and mission. These beings may also leave and be taken up to a certain level of glory to fulfill a mission, such as the City of Enoch.

I prepared these holy people with the same teachings I am beginning to give you. I am grateful they accepted and were willing to follow My teachings. This will be a great advantage when they return and will have a strong influence during the Zion time. Generally, these individuals will eventually *step out of their body* taking on a *similar* state of death though the body is not in a deteriorated state. Instead it is in a *suspended 'rest'* like a deep sleep or coma. Then the spirit will take up the body again into a higher glory.

Another way of not experiencing death is to move from a mortal state to an immortal state in the *'twinkling of an eye'*. This occurs when the spirit and body together, having never been separated, will be transported through a portal of Light to a heavenly realm, usually Celestial. On occasion, such a *being of immortality and eternalness* will also return to Earth and continue to be an influence but will have opportunities to move from realm to realm or kingdom to kingdom at will. Elijah is an example of such a person.

Even now, though I mention these ways of transitioning in life, I want you to know that **you need to pray and ask to have revealed to you your life plan.** All the different possibilities and ways of moving into Eternal Life are wonderful and divinely planned.

If there has not been the plan set in your personal Book of Life for by-passing death, *this is not denied to you*. Again, you may always choose. It is not restricted to anyone. Yet there must be a defined focus and much work to be accomplished. Not one step can be left out of the detailed learning that must take place for all the children of God as they progress to become like the Holy Parents. There are individuals who were prepared for a certain amount of overcoming, lessons to be learned, and missions to be accomplished. Though rare, some have completed all that was planned for them and can advance even further. If you choose a way of bypassing the normal death experience, it will require the utmost from you and yet *can be*.

There is never a restraint from the Father for your progression, and *My Atonement has taken your life not only through excellence for this life but also all the way forward to your complete exaltation to be a God*, even as the Eternal Mother and Father Elohim are. The fullness of My Gift is freely offered to all realizing there are the requirements as I have mentioned before.

Overcoming Death for the New World
Throughout time these options of overcoming death have not been emphasized greatly. To you and those who are seeking the greater way of being and are preparing for Zion, I am teaching and even emphasizing these extended ways of overcoming death. *Why now?* A certain number of individuals are needed to stay upon this Earth for her transition into an exalted state of Glory, even a Zion Glory. I have purposely placed individuals on the Earth at this time who are eternally advanced and prepared to receive the fullness of My Gift even to overcoming death.

At this point in time, I need for a certain number of people to hold this power to overcome death because the Fullness of My Atoning Gift must be received to create the greater Light and higher vibration of glory for transitioning into Zion and My Millennial Reign. We cannot have the spirit of death in the New World when I arrive. This fallen nature cannot be upon this planet when I come; it must be removed. You must recognize the deceptions, lies, and deterioration of understanding, which have caused death. This sham has been introduced subtly and craftily by those who have been influenced by the dark one. Death is contrary to what we are, as God-kind. We are living beings. The very fact that you are of God, our *Eternal* Mother and Father, naturally makes you *eternal*. Ultimately everyone[4] will receive the fullness of life in an eternal, glorified state.

Because of a person's life plan, some will stay and be here when I come again. For those whose plan is to overcome death there is something I want you to understand; it is still up to you to choose. Your original life plan is not a concrete, rigid obligation. I am going to say that again. *To receive the fullness of My Gift, it is not a requirement I put upon you to overcome death while still in the body, though it is a fabulous option.* If you have lived in worthiness and are to be here during Millennial time, yet have gone through death, this can still be. There are resurrected beings who will return and be here during that time. Some of those will descend with Me when I do return in Glory. Ah, such a *glorious* day; look forward to that day with Me.

Without question, the level of transition to overcome death takes *tremendous* effort on the person's part, too, so that we may accomplish this great and magnificent plan. It takes total devotion; it takes much prayer and willingness to change. It takes a *complete* letting go of all

---

[4] This, of course, is with the desire of the individual. Sometimes a being, once an offspring of God, may choose to relinquish that birthright because of individual will and agency. This must be an option because God honors agency.

fallen nature *and* stepping out of the lesser and lower ways of the world. There are some luring aspects of Satan's polished up, artificial ways that are very enticing and 'comfortable' once established, but all those seeming benefits are fake and have superficial payoffs. You must see these ways for what they really are and move magnificently into a greater and more glorious way of living.

It is offered to you to go through the exercise of learning how to reverse death and fallen nature. You need a teacher for this. I am here to teach you how to do that completely. I have created the transitioning and elevating of your particular experiences, body, and life. Your spirit has already been taught about resurrection and how to overcome all the deceptions and death causing distortions. You now need to learn with Me, placing into physical reality what your spirit knows. An important part of My Gift is to restore what you have already been taught, helping to remove all of Satan's influences and restore your eternal, true nature. If your path is to go through a death, you can be ready for a quick turnaround. Either way, let's do as much on this side as we can. *This is My ideal I offer to you.*

Life Plan Reality on Earth

It is important to pray and come to know what your life plan is and to receive a confirmation and testimony of it. This can be quite a project and because of the immensity of the task, it will take time and many prayers as I prepare you to know more who you are, your life lessons, and your mission. I will be with you and guide you on this assignment.

All ways of entering into eternal life are honorable. When I asked my disciples what their desire was, all except one chose to be with Me and the Father in our Heavenly Kingdom. Their desires were righteous. Yes, I was also greatly pleased with the desire of My disciple John. Because of his love for Me, he wanted to stay on Earth and continue to bring others to Me and the Father. There will be some of you who will desire this, too. It is already in the life plan for some; for others, it is not. Still, as I have said, you may choose to add this to your life plan.

Some will believe they have a life plan to overcome death, but it may not be so. They may have falsely determined this out of pride. Overcoming death may seem or be promoted as 'tantalizing' as if it is the 'higher' way. *This is a misunderstanding.* This way is not superior. One will not gain more glory by coming into eternal life without going through a death. People who enter into this prideful desire and put their effort into it, deny themselves of the very goal they desire. You must also beware of pride even if your life plan is to transition into eternal life without a death. This is why I ask you to work closely with Me so you can know the life plan for you and accomplish it honorably.

If choosing to overcome death isn't in your life plan, you *could* choose it now. We never limit. However, many *think* they can *simply* alter the plan. The intention and desire must be pure and the revision must be *without any* of the aspirations for their own glory, to think this is a better way or *just* to serve mankind. It is vitally important to understand that when they attempt to make a new life plan, they must absolutely do so out of their love for the Father.

That love must be *very pure* and their will must be *aligned* with the will of the Father. *Then* they may be granted this opportunity to have a new life plan that would include staying here upon Earth. Be aware this will include the reason of, yes, serving Me so that I may fully express My love along *with* you to the Father. This would please Me greatly. All the service I do is because I love the Father. Yes, I love mankind perfectly, but I love Heavenly Father and Mother first.

If you are to join *with Me*, on My mission, then you must love the Father as deeply and as thoroughly as I do *and* be willing to do His will. You *can* choose to change your life plan to include transitioning without death, but you must realize it is asking to alter a plan of the Father, Whose plans are perfect. Still, in that perfection, there could be different, honorable, alternative ways. The Father's wisdom is perfect. Though a perfect plan has been made, the ways to accomplish your mission and lessons are 'rearrange-able' as to how they will be fulfilled. Even though We may offer that you can stay, it is necessary for you to be willing to surrender *if* it is the greater wisdom of God's will that you come home.

Humility and Surrendering to God's Will

It is very important that you have a pure love of God, to be completely willing to surrender to whatever is God, the Father's will. The original life plans were not made casually, but were very carefully designed. Our Father has greater wisdom, far beyond ours. Again, I say there are many beautiful ways to enter into eternal life. I honor them all. One can certainly have a pure love for God and be desirous to go home.

Regardless of what your life plan is, it takes a true decision with determination and considerable time with Me for the maximum results to be fulfilled in your plan. Ah, but dear one, the results are so worth all that you may seem to give up in return for My restoring and lifting you to the holiest life which is beyond the description of any words I could use.

The spirit of humility is vital to support one in all aspects of their life's mission. Pride can feel satisfying when there is an influence and an apparent power over others. Pride can also be a false sense of worth from one's accomplishments and mastery in some aspect of life. The accolades of the world applaud loudly and have much glitter and appeal. *True* humility is really an honest knowing of one's self. It is an awareness of where you are in your personal progression towards coming completely to God. Ultimately, being children of God, your greatest triumph is to be as God, our Eternal Parents. Strangely enough, some will think this a prideful idea. A humble people do not think lowly of themselves nor do they exalt and think greater of themselves than what truly is the reality. Again, it is an honest knowing of yourself and does *not* include *any comparison* to others, just to God. Ask, my dear friend, to have Me fill you with the true spirit of humility. It is actually liberating, refreshing, and empowering; it is pleasing to God.

Embrace Life Fully
Let these thoughts sink deeply into your being. It is important for you to pray and ask for inspiration as to your particular life plan about transitioning from a mortal life to an immortal one. Have an inner discussion with your spirit. What do you *really* choose? What does your heart tell you? Let's begin now in great earnest to bring you forth to your highest plan, what your soul longs for, and what you really desire.

Oh, I would that you completely understand and embrace with your whole soul what I have said to you. The subtle refinement of your specific exaltation will come only by our personal relationship, yours and Mine. Let's transform, improve, and refine even the tiniest of details in your feelings, thoughts, and beliefs. It is vital and important that we have Sacred Time together. Please, receive a testimony of what I have presented. This will help us to move forward to the ultimate for which this writing is intended. *Please, dear one, come now; it's time for prayer.*

Alive in Christ – *The Gift*

Chapter 8

The Keys of Love, Gratitude, and Praise

My great desire is for you to open yourself up and allow the Love that I have for you to fill your being until you recognize and experience it. You may be used to reading My words that I have sent through my servants. However, when you read these written words, you may not realize that this is intended to be just like hearing My voice, as if I were sitting next to you. I *personally* send you this message in written form. It is meant to be personal, just the two of us, and I am speaking directly to you with My Light radiating out, sending out the Love I have for you through the printed word. Perhaps you have heard individuals who have experienced passing through the veil and being in My presence expressing how exquisite the experience felt. That experience is also to be for you, and it is to be here upon this Earth!

Your divine commission has not been clearly taught on Earth. My message is that you are to have the veil parted and allow the division between us to be *transitioned.* What I greatly desire is to pour forth from the Heavens the same Light and Love that exists there and bring it here upon Earth. It was My great prayer: "*Let it be done on Earth as it is in Heaven.*" The fullness of this can only be done by having the veil parted and connecting Heaven with Earth. That is part of your mission; and it is part of Mine.

Feeling the Presence of God's Spirit
What is it like in the Heavens? Feeling the presence of God's Spirit is the beginning, and you have had moments when you have felt the Divine move upon you. A wide variety of terms are used to describe the sensation or the quiet knowing within you that says: *Whatever is being heard, whatever thoughts are present, or whatever the moment is about, there is something holy . . .* that is Divine Presence. In that moment when you are spiritually seeing, feeling, hearing, or knowing, that sensing is real, and it is just as valid as your physical senses. You are connecting to a dimension that exists, to a place greater than this physical world.

Truly there is a spiritual world. Truly there is a Heaven. Truly there is Divine above. There is a Divine Father, and however you experience Him, however you experience Divinity, it is the deliverance of energy and of Love that allows you to sense what is beyond the five physical senses. This holy connection you have at that moment is a personal awareness of your relationship with the Heavens which can expand until it becomes constant in every moment of your life. What can stay with you beyond the experience is your testimony of such, however you express it. You may say: *I felt the Spirit move upon*

Chapter 8 – The Keys of Love, Gratitude, and Praise

me. I was stirred within. There was a burning in my bosom. I was filled with the knowing.

Many different words would describe such moments. In these moments you expanded your ability to experience a greater degree of Light beyond your normal capacity. Everyone, without exception, has a connection to the Heavens. There is a personal beam of Light, your own telephone line, if you will, connecting the Divine Mother and Father to you. This *Light of Christ*, as it is sometimes called, is God's Love kept accessible through My Holy Work, and it is kept open regardless of your performance. This Light that I keep constantly flowing is not only for your guidance but is also God's Love which supports your life.

Sometimes these 'moments of enlightenment' expand according to how you respond. They are intended to be the beginning of something greater. When you feel these surges of spiritual Light, usually a feeling of hope bursts forth upon you; your mind begins to expand in understanding, or joy fills your heart. Very often, perhaps if you have previously been in a situation, a problem, or an unknown, a new thought will come into your mind, and you are illuminated with greater understanding, with purer emotion, and the Virtues of Love such as patience, hope, gratitude, and harmony expand in you.

You may at one moment feel a stronger awareness of one particular divine emotion than at other times. For example, you may feel deep peace come upon you. You may feel exhilarating joy. You may feel deep gratitude that even moves you to tears. At these spiritual moments, your physical body is not generating these things by its own creation. These are manifestations of your spirit receiving an increase of Divine Love from the Holy Parents. This comes because of the expansion of your opening. Let's say at first you have a one-inch opening. Then, when your thoughts and emotions are brought to the Divine while in prayer, you have a 10" opening, or 20", or 30", and so forth. I use the numbers only to give an example. Just like your eyes slowly adjust to a brightly lit room, you also adjust to certain levels of Light from Heaven. This certain level of Light then becomes the norm until the Light becomes brighter and the eyes have to adjust again. It is the same spiritually as it is physically.

The Divine Eternal Substance of Love
In the interactions you have and all the work you do in the world—working with your family, working with other people, in prayer, your occupation, or any task—you are doing *spiritual work* because you are using a Virtue which is the Divine Eternal *substance* of *Love*. Whether aware of it or not, you are always using Divine Light and Love.

The very beautiful purer light and higher vibrations that come from the Heavenly source—the Love from the Mother and the Father for you—enhance your spiritual qualities and all activities. This spiritual Light enhances the spiritual work you do in the physical body, and it enhances, expands, nourishes, and feeds your spirit. Your spirit being needs this Light as food to continue to exist. *Emotional activity is similar to spiritual activity and also uses this Light, Love, and Truth.*

Your body is made of the elements of the Earth. Part of your natural human energy comes from the vibration of the earth and is inherently in your physical body. Within this innate physical structure is a capacity to produce energetic vibrations in interacting with the Earth. Physically moving your body puts into activity this innate generating and regenerating of energy. You gather additional energy and nutrition from the food that you eat, the water that you drink, the sunlight that shines upon you, the breath you take, and a multitude of other physical things that can enhance the physical body. You also need sleep in order to regenerate. You basically understand this.

In addition, all of your physical senses and capabilities also need spiritual Light as a source of energy. This energy is somewhat different from physical energy, and both spiritual and physical energy are needed by your body. Light energy is delivered along the spiritual path of your connection to God, the Eternal Mother and Father. Their Divine Light comes into your spirit body and then on into your physical body. Equally, by the additional Light or increase of energy from your spirit being, you also have an increase of energy in your physical body's vitality and sense of wellbeing. It is My responsibility to deliver Their Divine Light to you for your sustaining.

Fed and Energized from Two Different Sources

Emotional activity is similar to spiritual activity and also uses this Light, or Love and Truth. All of your physical senses and your mental and emotional activities and capabilities need spiritual Light as a source of energy. As you do more physical, emotional, and mental activities, you will use more Divine Light, as well as the energy from physical resources. So you are really being 'fed' and energized from two different sources.

Similar to the physical body, your spirit is divinely designed with innate energy and also needs an additional spiritual Light source for energy to function and keep on functioning. Spiritual activities use a spiritual source of energy—the pure, higher vibration which comes only from the Divine. These spiritual qualities enhance both the spiritual and emotional activity in your physical being, as well as expand, nourish, and feed your spirit.

Please realize that when you feel depleted and lack energy, you need to replenish not only with physical sources of energy but you also need spiritual food. Your need for energy cannot be met sufficiently just from physical source alone. When you feel you are going to 'lose it,' you need spiritual Light and fuel. Next time you are mentally, emotionally, or physically exhausted, come and turn to the Divine Eternal source for the energy you need.

The Divine Eternal Source

Again, My responsibility is to maintain the basic level of Light to sustain your spirit and keep your connection to

God. Your spirit is in a different place than it was when in your Heavenly home. Your spirit is still hungry for greater 'food', more Light. It is seeking for the Light that was experienced in Heaven before you were born into this body. You have had Divine Light before. The vibrant light, the Love, the energy, the power, and the magnitude of that Heavenly world are much greater than what you now experience in this world.

You were sent here to bring Heavenly Light into this earthly sphere. This starts with bringing greater Light into you. Greater illumination is needed for this task. A greater amount of 'food'—the nourishment from the Light and Love of Mother and the Father—is to be brought into your spirit to support both spiritual and physical activities. When you are completely filled with their Divine Light and Love, there is harmony in your physical being. The beautiful thing is the creation of the capacity not only to use Light for Divine purposes but also to multiply your own personal spiritual energy and power. This capacity to hold Light in your spiritual and physical beings is intended to continually increase. The greatness—in any and all types of manifestations in this world—increases the capacity of your spirit and physical beings to hold Light.

When you ask for and receive extra Divine energy and light for a purpose, you will receive a blessing of increased Light which can be expressed as an inspired thought, a boost of hope, or an increase of power in some manner. Your spiritual connection is enhanced. Remember, I explained this Divine Light can come forth and be used for all physical activities. For example, if a child is caught under a rock in a cave, you would pray and say: *God, help! Give me extra strength!* Your Holy Parents will immediately send in a source of energy for additional physical strength. Your physical body is also working to produce extra energy and strength. You most likely will also feel fear, panic, or worry. At this moment, the more that you turn your awareness to your love for this child and for God, the more you will be able to receive the peace, Love, light, and power that They are sending, which will amplify the strength in you and help you to remain calm and lift the rock.

If you have a strained situation with a co-worker or friend, you may pray and say: *Lord, I am feeling stressed and anxious. Please help me to feel peaceful and calm.* At that moment, again, there will be a deliverance of increased Divine Energy, Light, and Love from God for emotional strengthening so that you may stabilize your feelings. Then you are in a much better situation to think clearly and be inspired to know how to best move forward. The more you turn to Divine Source, the greater your capacity will be to receive and utilize this additional power in all aspects of your life.

There are times when you do not have information that you need. You are praying and asking for an answer: *Guide me. I do not know. I do not understand this.* At that point, you can receive an increase of this beautiful, Divine Light which will flow into your mind to bring forth a new thought, or understanding, or an illumination of ideas. Sometimes this flow of spiritual energy will flow out into the world to bring to you the support or answer you desire, from an outside source. It is still all from God.

Spiritual work such as an ordination, a blessing, a healing, or any of the other Gifts of the Spirit are all using spiritual energy. Yes, they use physical energy drawn from the energy sources of the world and the physical body's capacities, and they also definitely use spiritual energy—the Divine Love and Truth from the Eternal Mother and Father. *All spiritual energy comes from the Holy Divine Source* and is placed into your being to bring forth that spiritual deliverance so you may do something that is beyond the norm in the physical world. This capacity can and is intended to increase in you. The great spiritual ones in history were individuals who continually drew forth and righteously used the power source of Divine Light. This Light increased in them and brought forth Miracles—something done far beyond the natural laws and ways of this world.

How You Multiply Spiritual Energy

You not only use Divine Light but you also multiply it. How can this power become stronger in you so you experience more evidence of power in your life? How is it that you multiply it? How is spiritual energy not depleted but instead multiplied? It is done with *gratitude*. It is done with a return of honor and praise to the Heavens above. This returns this divine energy back to its origin. You give back with your gratitude and prayers of praising, adoring, and expressing the love you have for your Heavenly Mother and Father from your heart.

As Gratitude circulates between you and Mother and Father, it multiplies. The spirit of Gratitude also increases in you. This increases all the goodness and capacities you have. When you express gratitude for the extra physical strength that came because of the Divine Light, your physical body's strength becomes even more than it was before. When you express gratitude for the peace and calm you have prayed for, you will experience an increase. When you return in gratitude, the new and brighter Light not only stays with you but also increases. All blessings of any kind will increase with expressed gratitude to the Divine Ones. Gratitude is the key for all increase and abundance of everything good.

As you express gratitude, *all of the Virtues, all of the strength in your physical body, and all of the illumination of your mind will be sustained and even multiplied by the spirit of gratitude and praise to your Eternal God.* You open up the full circuit of connection, inviting their Light and Love to flow in and increase. Bring your heart and your thoughts in reverence and adoration for your Holy Heavenly Parents. They are the source of all that you are and everything that you have. Give gratitude back to Them. They will give back to you, everything increased and multiplied. They are not just necessarily sending you more; you also become the creating multiplier. Oh, how My soul rejoices in such gratitude and the increase of connection and multiplying of all that is good!

Chapter 9

I Will Come and Be Before You

I am here to open up the Heavens to you. I am the conduit for that, and I hold this position. Your part is to continue on a regular basis to express gratitude for this beautiful home here, for the life you do have, for your Heavenly Parents, and for Our Love. *When your spirit is illuminated with the fullness of My Being, I will come and be before you.*

While reading this message, some people who have read stories of others being exposed to My presence might ask: *Well, did they work this hard upon it? Did they pray mightily as much as I do? I have heard that they had not, but that it came from simple experience.* Sometimes certain individuals need to have a spiritual experience such as Paul of the New Testament. For some, such spiritual experiences are necessary to sustain or awaken them, adding dimension to their lives. In return, without exception, they are to bless others, testify of truth, and bring people closer to God.

Sometimes there are individuals who have had a very Divine experience—even visitations from angelic beings and the hosts of Heaven—who still stay upon their deviating course and do not praise and honor and love the Heavens above. For these individuals, their experience will stand as a testimony against them. Also, some who have holy missions have not yet had this kind of spiritual experience though they have prayed mightily.

I ask that you seek not just to have a spiritual experience, but instead, seek to glorify the Eternal Ones then all experiences will come to you in the wisdom of God's timing. Yet, when it does come upon you—and it will come—when the veil is parted, there will be no division between you and the Heavenly realm. This experience that you will have—the continual opening of the view into the Heavenly realm and communication with Me—will be measurably expanded beyond even some of the stories you may have heard. It will not be temporary. It will be on a constant, ongoing, daily basis. My energy and My being will be continually present with you. I intend for this to be experienced by many more individuals than have experienced this in times past.

This connection to the Heavenly realm is vital for My leaders who will create Zion and My New World. The time is now for the greater linking of Heaven and Earth. This is My intention and plan. To accomplish this you will also need to join with Me and do your part. I ask you to choose this with all your heart and soul, dedicating much time and energy with Me, bringing righteousness into every moment of your life.

You may wonder how I can be present with you and so many others on a daily basis. When a vibration from My Being is sent forth, there is no separation between us, the frequencies between you and Me make such a strong connection that no matter where I am, I see you. This is to become two-way. I have the capacity to echo My energies out to you in such a manner as to create a personal conversation and interactive experience between us.

I speak of things that may seem unreal to you, a *fairy tale*, a story in a book, something from long ago, something imaginary and not real. As I said at the beginning, as you read these words I would that you feel and hear in your heart and mind what I am saying as if I were standing before you speaking, so you hear Me directly, and feel My love. Please continue to pray and ask for a testimony of what I express to be a reality for you.

On Earth as it is in Heaven

I am calling you to fulfill My prayer to "Let it be on Earth as it is in Heaven" where there is no division, where there is holiness here on Earth as it is in the Holy Kingdom of the Mother and the Father. Love does abound there, and gratitude, hope, harmony, peace, joy—every good virtuous thought and feeling. Yea, every Truth does exist there, and it expands at all times.

Goodness and light exist in the Heavenly home where I now dwell. Are there many places within this Heavenly home? Yes. Are there different degrees of Light? Yes. They all hold a spirit of righteousness. Just as you can increase the light in a room to be brighter, so there is more light, so it is in the different degrees of Glory, the different places in our Heavenly Home. They who reside therein hold pure goodness, Love, and Light, and are constantly increasing in knowledge and in all the virtues. There is improvement among people in their ability to comprehend, connect, and communicate. There is continual progression. *Those in the Heavenly realm may transport to be in any place that exists in equal or lesser degrees of Light or Glory.*

Your Being is to Be a Portal to Heaven
This is the time when we are to draw this entire planet upward. Its vibration and glory are to increase. There is currently a physical rearrangement of the planets and heavenly bodies which is now creating a new frequency. Portals of light between Our Heavenly Mother and Father and the inhabitants upon this Earth are being created and are increasing. *Your being is to be a portal to Heaven* to bring increased Light into this world!

A certain level and purity of light frequency are required for all who will remain here upon this planet. Those who do not reach this level will not be able to abide the light that is to be here. It will be too much for them. They will be taken to a place—a Heavenly place in its own way—and prepared, outside of their physical bodies, for their further development. Eventually, they will take up their bodies again, experience a resurrection, and move on in their spiritual progression. Those who will remain here upon this Earth in its physical state in their physical bodies will need to experience a *transformation*. This transformation will come to you by opening up daily to the Heavens above and giving gratitude and praise to your God. This will increase the level and purity of your light frequency!

This information is not just words for you to read. If you will choose to have it be, the meanings can be delivered to you with Light through the personal channel that connects you to your beautiful Holy Parents. We are delivering this Truth not only in words but also by the vibrations and the Love that attend and nurture these words. Allow this deliverance by being in a prayerful state as you read. Come, be in prayer, express your gratitude and love that you will have these multiply in you and not just read information with emptiness. Let the words grow and be alive in you! *Love the words! Love the Truth! Love the Divine Ones!* Let your mind and your heart rejoice together! Let the possibility enter!

If you have any doubts, say: *I would desire to have this. I am at least open that this is a possibility for me. As I grow and continue to experience increasing Light in me, this might be a reality for me.* This is a start. Do you desire it? Yea, I know that you do. Then let your desire grow! Let your desire grow by feeling the love for every good thing that exists! Feel your love for the Mother and the Father! Feel your love for yourself! Feel your love for others! Feel your love for this glorious and beautiful Earth! Express gratitude for every good thing that is in your life! Then the gratitude for any one particular thing will *increase*.

All Virtues and All Truth Will Expand in You

At the same time, your gratitude will increase your love overall. All virtues and all truth will expand in you as you send back gratitude for your Eternal Mother and Father who have created all. Express your gratitude for the myriad of physical materials and objects which have been created to provide for and sustain your physical life, as well as to bring you delight. Gratitude and love will grow every good thing within you! Your works will be stronger. Every part of you will continue to increase.

Some have experienced physical healing. Some have experienced even a *miraculous* healing, which they recognized. Whether by prayer, by laying on of hands, by blessings, or whatever— they have experienced a mighty change in the physical body. Oh, that they would continue on with the *praising and glorifying God, even every day*! For often some will say at the beginning when the healing or blessing has come forth: *I am so grateful for that blessing. Thank you*! But then they go on their way and do not sustain the gratitude.

Let there be a *continuation* of gratitude every day for physical things. It does not mean that you need to list every single blessing you've ever received. Just bring forth a sampling of what your heart feels gratitude for: this beautiful physical world, your amazing physical body, your glorious Heavenly Parents who are the Divine Source of the very love and life that you hold within you. Give praise and honor and glory to Them daily. Come in prayer and be with Me also. Come talk to Us. Open yourself up on a continual, everyday basis. May the spirit of gratitude and praise fill your being and multiply within you continually.

Often there are those who will attend church, a seminar, a presentation, or read a book, which has a beautiful message that stirs their souls. They say: *That was a wonderful message*! They may even feel a determination to be a better person. How sad it is in reality that they often do not remember to come back in prayer and gratitude—a true, genuine, sincere, from-the-heart-and-mind gratitude— for the beautiful message. Gratitude empowers each of us to live these messages and begin to multiply those very words, the very thoughts, the very message itself. Gratitude empowers us to be part of this multiplication process. Please, give more gratitude in *sincerity*. Give more praise and honor and love for the Holy Divine Ones.

My Invitation for You
Gratitude multiplies and increases all good things. It brings an increase of Light which continues to illuminate first your spirit being, then your physical being. Gratitude fills you with an increase of Light in the body, in the mind, in the emotions, in the physical structure, and in your spirit. You can increase your ability to be in constant praise for the blessings of God in every thought and

every emotion. Everything that you do can be filled with praise, honor, glory, and gratitude, continually renewing and replenishing you. The very spirit of praise and gratitude is to be woven naturally into everything you do. You may find yourself going about a task feeling very happy without consciously telling yourself to be happy—you just are. *This is the way it can be with you*—holding this natural spirit of gratitude and praise to God during all that you do.

When you return gratitude and honor to God, there is an immediate return back to you. It is beautiful when you also hold the spirit of gratitude for there is an immediate return and increase of Light and Love. In any moment when you might need physical strength, a healing, some emotional stability, or illumination of your mind, please remember, the Divine Ones are with you. As you open and express gratitude, you will receive the greater of God's Light so you never feel stressed, worried, or anxious. Those negative emotions would not close you down or make you physically less capable of receiving the necessary Light, Love, and Truth to give you the additional strength and power that you need. My reaching out to you in this book has a major purpose, *to let you know how close We are and how much We desire to bring you forward into greater life.* Please come to know how much more this can be.

This divinity can be developed within you, My precious one. Then you will be alive, *so fully alive*—more alive than at this very moment. This is what I have prepared for you now. I have received all from the Eternal Father and Mother, and I have prepared the deliverance to you of all that They are. When you are filled with the fullness of Love and Light, there is no division—you have Heaven in you. The Heavens can see you, and you can see the Heavens while also illuminating this world with your light and helping to bring this world to her greater glory.

More Divine Light is being presented to the world than ever before. I am opening portals to increase light to the entire world for any who seek for such and will receive it. You chose to read this book, and now you are more aware of what is taking place. Take advantage of this light and awareness by coming to develop our relationship and receive the greater that I have for you personally. This is the time—now!

The time until My coming draws short. *The number of people already on the Earth who will be present when I come is greater in number than those who will yet be born and be here for My Second Coming.* Therefore, I give you an invitation: Come, build Zion. Bring the Heavens into you by the increase of Light in you. Bring forth and develop a continual state of tender gratitude, praise, glory, and love within. Send these righteous ways of being to the Holy Ones above who will return to you even more until it is constantly one eternal round, flowing in and through you. It is your True Nature to always be in this constant state of love, joy, peace, gratitude, and harmony while praising and loving and adoring your Holy Parents.

Come, I Will Take You Unto Them

I am here to deliver this to you. Come, that you might know Me also, and I will take you unto Them in the fullness therein. Come, that we might bridge the gap. I reach down from the Heavens and extend My hand to you here upon the earth and say: *Come, come. Invite Me in. Let Me stand in your presence. Daily exercise yourself.* Make it a practice that you develop gratitude and that your thoughts throughout the entire day are lifted up by saying: *Thank you, My Holy Ones. I Love you. I adore you. You are glorious!* Express such praise even when there is nothing in particular in the physical world that has caused you to feel loving or joyful or grateful. Just feel the love that is naturally in your spirit and heart, the Love that They send into you. Oh, feel it! Open up!

Be still that you might feel the presence of Their Love and My Love for you and your love for Us. Let it extend out, and let all of your being—all of your heart, might, mind, soul, and with every bit of energy within you—send adoration, love, praise, and glory to your Holy Parents. Have time when all you do is feel that sweeping of Love coming down from Them and through you then back up to Them. *That is the most exquisite and beautiful of experiences.* Such experiences will thin the veil of separation until it is no more.

Come. Be fully alive in all that I have to deliver to you. Make room within. Expressing gratitude and love can be woven into your thoughts and activities throughout your day. Frequently praise and adore the Holy Ones who give to you, and have given to you, and will yet give to you even all things; even everything that They are and everything that They have. *I know this to be true, for the Father has given Me all that He is and all that He has. I come to extend it out to you.*

Oh, bring this up as a priority of your life, dear precious one! These sweet fruits will return unto you. Be ye in the constant joy of harvesting their Love even more than in the anticipation of the fullness of the fruits. Be ye in the joy of praising, and the fruits will part the veil between Heaven and Earth naturally. Set not so much the goal in mind, but find the joy of just loving Them, loving Them, *loving Them!* Then know that the parting of the veil will be. It will be. *It will be.*

Be patient for the fruit of the Tree of Life and the fullness of the Light that you are. Let this take its natural course to expand. Hold faith and trust. Trust that the time is sufficient. As you take advantage of every day to increase your love for God, I shall deliver illumination unto you, every day so that your physical being has increasing capacity in the daily ability to be a container for God's Love and Light. Be ye, therefore, filled with the Holy pattern that returns adoration and praise to the Heavens above.

This is a beautiful time in which you live. Oh, *precious one*, recognize what an honor has been given to you! What a cherished sacred space and moment in all of the Earth's existence! You are not only here upon the Earth for these grand culminating events, but you are also here to receive the knowing, the testimony, the burning within you of spiritual understanding of what you have been taught, and of the spiritual experiences that you have had, and that you are yet to have. *What a Divine blessing this is!* Recognize it! Be in gratitude for it! Thus it will grow and multiply in you.

Let Us praise Our Holy Parents forevermore! They are the Source of all life! They are the Origin of Eternal Life! I have received it, and I am prepared to deliver it unto you. Oh, My precious one, go forth and rejoice in that! This is the good news! This is Eternal Life, and it is offered to *YOU*.

My Request

I am asking you to remember to read this carefully and slowly. There is a tendency when there is no new information, to skim over the words looking for something *substantial*. If people had stopped on the words, *Come unto Me* and really pondered this, felt My Spirit calling them, felt My deep love, My willing desire to work with each person, there would be a much more profound influence and more results from my call.

There are places in this book where I ask you to choose some way of being and work with Me so we can make your miraculous transformation. Please, honor My request. I asked at the beginning of this book to please stop and pray frequently throughout the book. *I remind you, I am aware of everything you do.* When you do not pause your reading to pray, it is the same as *ignoring* Me, though I asked while standing right next to you. I remind you again, this is not just a book. I am speaking to you.

Please, read and pray often so the spirit in the words can open and bless you and My message can be fully delivered. Then I can work with you as I have intended. I so desire for you to experience the Love I have for you.

Alive in Christ – *The Gift*

Chapter 10
Ultimate Spiritual Awareness

My dear one, I am so grateful you have made time today to sit down and read My message to you. I know sometimes it may not be easy to find the time to quietly do so. I am keenly aware of what is going on everywhere and even of every situation in your personal life. I am deeply grateful when you take the time to read and ponder and take a moment to pray for us to be together.

I am asking you to please increase your Sacred Time with Me. This time can include a song, scripture study, and listening to messages of a spiritual nature. Yet it must also include direct conversation, prayer filled with praise and worship to God. Express what is in your heart. Let this time include conversations between us, working with Me to recreate new patterns in your body, and visualizing what you desire to bring into your life. Be still to receive and ponder your thoughts, your impressions, and what you are experiencing.

Through this Sacred Time, you will develop a keener awareness of life. I desire for you to develop a greater capacity within you. I am fully aware of everything, and I desire to give unto you all that I am: to transfer to you the higher, spiritual Light and to activate your dormant, spiritual qualities. This activation in your physical being can only be completely experienced with the Light from Me. You have the innate capability to be much more aware of what is going on even beyond what your mind and physical senses normally perceive. The progress may be very subtle at first yet the potential for Godly excellence is in you.

Developing Your Spiritual Awareness

At the beginning, you are not going to be aware in the same degree that I am, for I am aware of what is taking place all over the world with every single individual. This degree of awareness is also your potential. You certainly can begin to be more aware of the first energy transmissions of what is going on with the individuals you deal with—the person you are interfacing with or are thinking about at that moment. It is possible to have your mind think about particular individuals, someone that you love and care about, and, as you take a few moments just to pause, you can begin to sense what is going on in them and their lives. Perhaps this awareness is of the overall condition, a sensing that things are going well or not, or a sensing that things are exceptionally busy in their life, a sensing that things are in turmoil, or a sensing that things are very quiet. At first, your awareness may not hold any detail, though sometimes some very vivid thoughts will come to your mind about their situation. When you do this for the purpose of good and to love and support another person, your ability will increase.

Many different impressions, thoughts, and emotions may come into your being. At first, they may be subtle. Your mind is used to trying to figure out everything by using your five senses and reasoning. Questioning and doubting spiritual impressions come easily. When you receive an impression or thought, work with your mind and say: *Let us just suppose that maybe, just maybe, this is accurate; at least it is a possibility.* Somehow the mind is more comfortable with considering a possibility. This opens up observing and noticing the energy and impressions rather than trying to figure things out from what you might already know of conditions and situations in another person's life. *This ability to be able to tune in to other people must be based on a desire to add goodness to their lives. It cannot hold any purpose to manipulate, interfere, or control.*

Being aware of someone else and picking up that subtle knowing about them helps you to attune to receiving Divine inspiration, guidance, and revelation for yourself, as well as helping you to tune in to other people to be able to best support and interface with them. In a very basic way, you have experienced this at one time or another. Think back to moments when you have been with somebody, and right away you just sense something is disturbing them. They do not even have to speak a word; you just know. You are sensing the energy around them, and this is a good way to begin to honor your natural spiritual ability of awareness. Tuning in to another person's life for righteous purpose supports the ability to tune in to spiritual energy which is all around and within your being. In fact, spiritual energy is subtle energy, though not all subtle energy is spiritual Light energy.

Impressions Sent To You by Heavenly Beings

Being aware of subtle energy ties into sensing the *impressions sent to you by Heavenly Beings* who work with you: angels of Light, the Holy Spirit, God the Eternal Father and Mother, and Me. We are all acutely aware of what is going on in your life and are able to send you impressions to support and guide you, depending on what you are dealing with at the time. Sometimes We add to your impressions from subtle energy to enhance what you already know.

There are reasons why I am teaching you this. It ties in with becoming more Alive and vital in Me. To be *Alive in Christ* is to be more alive in yourself, to be more keenly aware of *your* senses, and to experience an expanding increase of *your* capacities. What I would desire is to deliver unto you more of your innate, divine capabilities; adding more Light and Love to nourish and develop these spiritual capabilities your physical body has.

In all of the many things which are going to take place in your life, it will be highly beneficial for you to develop this innate, divine quality of awareness which every person has deep within. This spiritual awareness is very much in your innate potential, though it is usually not fully developed and may only come, in part, with the refinement that develops later in life. Just like a child learning to write, the finer muscle skills are not developed until later. At first, though they are using their muscles, some muscles are simply not as refined, not as attuned to the capabilities that will eventually come. *I desire to give to you the greater offered Light so this innate divine nature of yours can be fully developed and thus prepare you for the greater power that your life can have.*

Bypassing Diversions

In this world, there is much confusion to deter you from developing this refined innate sense of awareness. One diversion is that your mind has been trained and exercised to be responsible and to be in control. It has also been embedded with a compulsion to be right. The world teaches that the mind should be in charge and that it is the ultimate source to solve problems and come up with solutions. Most believe the mind is the origin of creation. Individuals have been revered, celebrated, and even worshiped for their great intelligence. This exalting of intellect has been passed down through all generations.

Another diversion is the pattern of your emotions being the controlling factor in your decisions. Sometimes people, especially when they are emotional around a spiritual topic, believe they are also being spiritual. *This is not necessarily so.* Some people feel that because they are attuned to their emotions, they have a greater capability to be attuned to the subtle, spiritual energies. That also is not necessarily true all the time. In fact, sometimes when people are too influenced by their own strong emotions as a prominent leading force in their lives, these strong emotions can *drown* out the more spiritual, subtle energies that are given to guide and direct them.

Using Subtle Energy
Erase the belief that only a certain type of person has more capability than another to be in tune with spiritual energy. If you believe you are just not *the type* to be aware of the spiritual, it is simply not so. Everyone has the capacity to do this. It is a matter of practice and development. Take and make the opportunity to exercise yourself in much prayer and sacred time to expand your spiritual awareness. Take time to be still, listen, and notice.

Sometimes difficult experiences seem to entreat desperate people to seek spiritual help because there does not seem to be an alternative solution. As a result, some have developed a greater capacity to be open to inspired guidance and support because their circumstances have needed this Divine assistance. *They have learned to surrender their attempts to control and manage alone.* Instead, they work with God while also still giving their all. This creates a capacity to be in tune. Every person can develop these spiritual skills to discern Our spiritual guidance and to understand and *read* the subtle spiritual energies. All can reestablish their innate capacity to always work with Us in everything. This is a delightful way to live.

Very often people will pick up on what is going on in another person. They may understand the emotions in that person, for example, and use this to manipulate, control, or use unrighteous influence. It is just as unrighteous to allow yourself to be controlled by other people by using the information from their subtle energy, and make that the deciding factors in your own decisions. In this way, you abdicate your own agency to choose and decide for yourself.

A possible result to this imbalance can be to cut off the awareness and separate from others, thus feeling falsely free to make your own decision without the awareness of others. However, this approach may bring forth poor decision making without the benefit of any consideration for others.

The *ideal* situation is to be very aware of what you think, feel, believe, know, desire, and what you are choosing to create in your life *and* to be very aware of the same for others. The greater way to gain true wisdom, peace, and success in your life is by receiving through the five senses *and* adding the subtle energies' information. This is also an art and ability that *all* can develop to a degree of excellence.

Maintain the Love Factor

The ability to maintain *Love is the major factor in using spiritual Light energy righteously*. Your care for another person's well-being not only keeps things open and flowing but increases your capacity to discern accurately and increase spiritual Light. When you are angry, judgmental, or upset, you energetically shift and are no longer open to accurately discern and understand what is going on. *Negative emotions and energies only confuse and conflict the whole situation.* If somebody says something to you, and you feel tension about what they have said, what they are doing, or what they are feeling, then at that moment you are not in tune to your higher ability to best handle the situation. *Do whatever you can to step away, even if it is just mentally and energetically detaching, and pray to receive My Peace, Love, and Light.* Express your love to God until you are clear and feel the Love from God return. Only then will you be ready to love the other, sense the Light's inspiration, and discern a better way to move forward.

Now, what about our relationship, yours and Mine? Oh, My dear friend, how I yearn to have you feel the Love I have for you personally. In a fallen state you feel so little. What I feel about you and how I look upon you is with complete, open Love, which is inseparable from the Love of your Heavenly Parents. I say to you that when I speak, it is also from your Holy, Eternal Parents. We desire greatly to have the Love as it is in the Heavens completely return and to have you experience fully the beautiful relationship between us all.

So often it is taught in this world that if you do or do not do certain things, then you are under great disapproval and condemnation from God above. I say to you: *That is not quite the right wording.* It really is not. We completely and perfectly understand all of your actions, reactions, emotions, feelings, and thoughts. Though some of these thoughts and emotions are not in alignment with Divine way, I still understand and mercy is My nature. You are in a state of learning and moving through life, experiencing for yourself various ways to your greatest advancement. I also know the way to lead you back to the pure ways of God, bringing the greatest joy, peace, and love back into your life, even as it was before this life, and even greater.

Any other way would be harsh. Any other way would deprive you of your own beautiful learning and growth. God is not in the least tyrannical about what must be, and such a dictatorial way would take away from the very beautiful being that you are. The commandments are only invitations and directions to righteous and joyful living, giving you the freedom to create. You are a child of the Holy, Living God. Your true nature has the ability to choose, decide, and experience, then to choose again, and decide and experience again. In this way, you are learning to clarify what you really want to do, be, and create. This freedom is vital to the God-kind being that you are, and to your God-given right to continue to become your own beautiful, unique person.

The *judgment* of God is often spoken about, but judgment has been so misused that you do not understand His judgment. The judgment of God—My judgment and God, the Father's judgment being one—is an absolute, perfect awareness of every contributing factor coming into your life: every influence, everything that you are from within, all the decisions you have made, all the different experiences that you are having through thoughts and physical activities. You are trying things out. You are learning. We are completely aware of everything going on inside of you. We are completely aware of everything that is coming from others and from outside sources influencing you in some manner. We understand all of the pressures that push you this way and that. We understand how much effort you are making to stand up, to be correct, and so forth.

With that, We give complete open space for you to have your experience. At the same time, We are always sending Light and Love to you on a constant basis for you to bring in the Divine substance that fuels your whole being. Invite in Our Light and Love. Bring it in. Learn to recognize it. Learn to increase it. Learn how much you can do with it and how much this expands your power and capacity to create with Our beautiful Essence. You may use this holy Light in so many wonderful ways. Enjoy it and receive it, take it and divert it, convert it and change it! Use it up or multiply it. This is Divine holy power, and it is part of who you are.

The Essence of Love and Truth
In the previous chapter, you read about multiplying Light and Love by praising The Eternal Parents and expressing your gratitude and love to God and others. In this great earth experience, you are learning how to take this precious God Essence into your being in greater amounts, giving you greater life. This Divine Essence is

Chapter 10 – Ultimate Spiritual Awareness

the *fuel* to keep you going and gives power to every part of your life.

With death, the physical body is only laid down temporarily, but it will again be charged with that same beautiful, Divine Essence to restore every particle back into a holy form, which will be illuminated with *greater light than before*. You will not hold at that time any of the seeds of destruction that have been from the fallen nature. Your spirit and your body are to be united with this Eternal Light and Power. *This Holy Essence of Love and Truth is what brings Eternal Life.*

How you use this beautiful, Divine Love Essence in this life is *very* important. Remember, your world has taught you very well to make your decisions with the mind, and that the mind is the beginning of all that you create. Either that or people use their emotions to direct their decisions. Your decisions are keys to all you create in your life. I say to you: *True creation begins with the beautiful Divine Love and Truth Essence from the Eternal Mother and Father, through Me and into you.* This Essence sustains you at all times and is the pure energy source of all you are and do.

When you become more aware of the subtlety of this Love and Truth Essence, you will have a greater capacity for your whole body to receive and practice being in tune with the awareness of the Truth which is also expressed in the subtle energies that dwell within you. If you are very *noisy*—outwardly busy, active, thinking, responding—and do not take the time to be still, to notice, and consciously sense this Light within, you will tend to follow the opinions you already have, many of which still hold the distortions of fallen nature's wiles. Use your Divine Energy Essence to fuel your awareness and your actions. Then you may purify yourself of all these falsehoods. Connect and use this greater Divine awareness and wisdom that is also offered to you in the subtle energy from Divine Essence.

God's Light, Love, and Truth can feed inspired and enlightened thoughts and information into your conscious mind. *There is not a fact in this world that you cannot gather from the beautiful, Divine Love Essence that flows into your being.* This requires being quiet enough to be aware of the different thoughts that are created out of the truth within, flowing through you constantly. Again, the normal pattern of this world is to act out of what has already been established, the habits we have developed from the world's teachings and the patterns given to us as protocol dictated by others. We cannot create the *new world* in this manner! I cannot give you the greater way from the Gift I have for you. Every day is to be a new level of capacity greater than the day before, blessed with new thoughts and awareness and greater levels of Light and Love. This comes from God's Essence of Love and Truth.

Chapter 11

Respectful, Honest Conversation

In all that you are receiving from this outward world's influence, there is always the inward Heavenly influence to balance you, when you are aware of it. *I ask for you to come, be with Me and your Heavenly Parents and have Sacred Time.* I use this term, Sacred Time, to lead you into an experience beyond what is usually considered prayer. Yes, use beautiful words that you have been taught when they are truly an expression of your desires and inward soul, this is fine. However, *true prayer is a conversation— a respectful, honest, open, two-way conversation with those of Us in the Heavens.*

In the spirit of conversation, prepare to be quiet and listen, so Our responses and answers come. Our responses and answers can come in many different ways. Some of those ways are an impression of a thought, an idea, a concept, a direction, or words that enter into your mind. These can be very specific or an overall impression. It could be an emotion that sweeps through you. It could just be quiet, yet in the quiet you are allowing the spirit of Our Light to fill your being. This prepares the spirit of openness and awareness to receive further. This stillness primes you for new thoughts that are different from your old patterns of thinking. Being still in that moment of quiet does not need to be necessarily long. Sometimes just a moment of stillness is sufficient. Other times this quiet stillness can beautifully linger for quite some time. Take a breath and just trust.

Have you noticed that when people are asked a deep question, there is silence for a while? You perceive that they are searching their minds and thinking through the answer carefully. Since you want to understand what they might say, you listen very intently while waiting for them to speak. You are very still and open, waiting, watching, and even sensing what is going on in their minds. Whether you realize it consciously or not, you are very open at that moment and are gathering in *subtle* energy data. This is the same when in prayer; do not assume that nothing is happening when it is *quiet*.

While conversing with the Heavens in prayer, you are also to be still and quiet and listening very intently. You might not register in your conscious awareness any feeling of emotion or thought, but I will tell you, you have received. You have *heard* what We have to say. As you continue, you will find that what you have *heard* will eventually convert --as if translated-- into thought, words, or impressions in your conscious mind.

Our Light in your being is converted into subconscious instructions in the physical body. You may naturally find yourself reacting or responding in a certain way. Without consciously recognizing it, you will be directed to be somewhere, do something, or say something. Our Essence converts into emotional energy, and you find yourself innately responding in a very positive, peaceful, joyful, and loving manner. Your emotions have received the pure Love and Truth's message given to you. *The quiet and still part of Sacred Time is vital to your prayers and our two-way communication.*

Meditation is a very holy practice done in a wide variety of ways. A lot of expectations are attached to meditation concerning what this experience should or should not be. It is the same with prayer. There is a wide variety of how people pray and meditate. There is no right or wrong way. It is helpful to practice this ability to be quiet and still. In some ways, meditation is not much more than just an extended period of this deep listening in which you are open and practice receiving the subtle, spiritual energies. At the time, you might not have a conscious awareness of what is really happening.

The Holy Sacred Space Beyond Words
Sometimes unawareness is really an advantage because the mind will want to grab that thought and immediately connect it to all the previous similar thoughts. This constricts and can limit the new ideas I am giving to you. You may make conclusions before you have received all of the ideas Our Light has to give to you. Take time for

the spiritual energies to come; enter into that *holy, sacred space which is beyond words.* Enjoy being in this peaceful, quiet place, this place of meditation and stillness, this place of awareness of God's Presence.

Though I do not desire to give you an exact process for stillness, using relaxed breathing can help you calm and quiet the mind which helps you to be aware of the subtle energies from Divine. In such a serene state, the holy Love, Light, and Truth can increase and, in turn, will increase your tranquility and nourish your whole being. In this abundance of serene spiritual Light, the mind becomes clearer and more aware, the emotions more stable, and the physical body healthier. All this supports you to prepare yourself for the greater, holier sacred spirit I desire to give to you.

What You Have Not Heard—What You Have Not Seen
Exercising yourself in being aware of Divine's subtle energies will help you in the ability to receive and accurately interpret those subtle energies. *This practice and ability is the very same thing that will allow you to be more attuned to others.* When you are attuned to someone else, you will begin to sense what is going on in them, even beyond their words or outward actions or expressed emotions. Being cognizant of divine, subtle energies also helps you be mindful of your own thoughts and feelings. Most people think they know their own thoughts and beliefs—after all, they are the ones thinking them. I say there is much you do not yet realize even about yourself. I greatly desire to open you up to *hear what you have not*

heard before and see what you have not seen before within your own being.

Knowing oneself in depth is the foundation to understanding more about Truth and how to become these eternal ways in fidelity, and then wisely applying this understanding to what is really going on in another person, in you, and in life. Through the increase of the Light, you receive beautiful truth and knowing. You will become exercised, practiced, and skilled in developing the capacity to know how to interface with another and with yourself. You will create a beautiful, harmonious, life-expanding way of interaction that will benefit all concerned. That is when *the spirit of Love and Truth from your Holy Parents is being expressed in you.*

As Love flows into you from the Divine Ones above, and as you express love to God and gratitude for all things, this allows Their Love to multiply in you. This Love allows you to remain accessible to Truth as God would use it. Remember, the presence of Divine Love creates a connective way of interfacing harmoniously with all that goes on in the world.

Living in this higher manner will also allow you to live with acute awareness without *unrighteous* judgment. It will help you to best understand the situation and lovingly hold firm to Divine Truth. *Let God always be the third party in all interactions with others.* Our Holy Parents and I are aware of what each person is thinking, feeling, and choosing. God's judgment is righteous because of the perfect Love He has. His judgments are pure evaluations of where anyone is in his or her infinite progression and of how to best support each one in eternally advancing. Only with pure Divine Love can you make a *righteous judgment*, a necessary discernment of what is going on, and how to wisely interact with every situation—with people, with life.

The greatest outcomes and most harmonious communications come when you are completely connected and open with love for another, for yourself, and for God. That is what you are to strive for. It is an obtainable ideal. That is also what I desire for you. Again, My gift is to lift you to the *highest* living, even as it is in the Celestial Heaven.

Clarifying Your Responsibility
While you may have a keen awareness of another, of self, and of Divine Presence to guide your decisions, comments, and actions, the other person may not feel the harmony. Perhaps you are to make a stand, express a truth, or take an action as you see it to be. It is still very possible for others to not understand and to not feel the harmony because they are out of alignment with Truth. That doesn't mean you have not created harmony. When you are in alignment with yourself and with Me and the Divine Spirit of Love and Truth, you will be able to remain calm, peaceful, and harmonious in your own being even though others may be upset. When you do not feel this calm, you need to connect deeper to God and His Light and Love. Also, seek to make sure you are com-

pletely connected to self and others. The *formula* will be complete, and once again you will feel at peace.

The point I am making here is that your responsibility is to be fully open and aware energetically of all that is taking place with these three aspects: connection with God, self, and others. Sometimes other people are happy. That does not mean something is *wrong. Their response is not your responsibility. Neither is their happiness your responsibility. Your responsibility is to live in alignment with God,* the Spirit of Love and Truth, and be fully aware of yourself and others, then live in that Spirit of Love and Truth. The additional awareness from the spiritual dimension is always of great value and will be the factor to actually help your life be more righteous and easier overall. The new spiritual awareness blends and balances all situations.

You can have My Divine knowing. I am connected to the dimension of the future—your future. I have been able to experience exactly what it is like to live your life, to be inside of you with every thought, emotion, and feeling. Because in this, I *know* where you are going. I know the goodness that is within you. *It is only the incorrect beliefs of this world you still hold to that keep you from what I would give to you.* I will give you carefully planned steps, teaching you the intricate details of living in Light. Practice your patience and be willing to be thorough with Me as I move you carefully along each day, even each moment. Please, desire greater to be continually with My

Presence and Spirit. You and I together can bring forth the fullness of My Gift. Such joy this brings to Me.

Live in Continual Peace, Joy, and Love

I desire for you to be as I am, living in continual Peace, Joy, and Love; *this brings complete freedom.* It enables Me to work with you in a manner that I know will ultimately bring you the greatest growth and value of life. This brings Me and the Holy Parents great joy. This is Our mission. You may not be aware that as I am interfacing with you. I am actively sending energies into your spirit and physical being and creating a relationship experience between the two. Even though you might not be happy at that moment, My Harmony and Love is still being delivered to your spirit and is present.

I am actually with you whether you are aligned with Truth or not. As you become aware of My Presence in your life and as you learn to open up to that, you will find that it will help you align with Holy Ways. Eventually that will bring you more peace and harmony in your life. The ultimate is for you to *live in continual peace, joy, and love with My wisdom at all times* no matter what is going on in your life, no matter what the outside circumstances are.

I do offer this at all times. Hear me again: *I am aware of you and everything that is going on within you!* In every moment I am offering up My Love, My Light, and My Truth and pouring them into you. I am kindly and keenly always interfacing in your life. I am not distant. I am not interfer-

Chapter 11 – Respectful, Honest Conversation

ing either, but I am constantly there with the support of Love and Truth.

I would that you practice this ability and know it will grow. Yes, it may seem as if it grows slowly; nevertheless, it is expanding or being offered to you at all times that you might receive and feel that Love, especially in the quietness in our Sacred Time together. After a while, it will begin to pick up pace. Continue to practice picking up the subtle energies of others, yourself, and Me. Bring these three holy centers together into harmony. This is necessary to eventually live a beautiful life continually with unbroken peace, love, harmony, and joy. This is your true nature, your true way of being and living.

We are this Love. My desire is for you to experience that. Love expresses itself in many ways. It always has a center of peace and the expression of joy and harmony and all other possible virtues, all holy ways of being. Love, that Divine Essence of God, is also inseparable from Truth, and these two are the foundation of all that We are as God-kind.

Let this holiness of Our Being pour into your being as you practice the ability to receive every day. You will improve with this practice. Love and Truth will build within you and expand. I understand well that sometimes you think: *But I have been doing this for a long time.* You may not be aware that it has been subtly improving and increasing as you daily have Sacred Time and practice stillness and quiet. Learn to listen when you are in prayer because We *are* having a conversation with you. Also, in order to understand others clearly and to know yourself, practice being still for a moment and gather subtle energies and then add the spiritual energies from Divine. *The pattern of the world is to rush everything and to work from habits of yesterday rather than being fresh and new with each moment.* I am asking you to be in a spirit of new awareness in the moment and improve and increase your spirituality and divinity every day.

Power of Decision
This continual improvement does not mean you must *work harder* but rather place a sincere desire and *choose* with all of your being to work with Me to bring this to pass. Too often you take this task of improving upon yourself *alone.* There needs to be a firm commitment in you for your improved relationships with others. There needs to be a *firm, absolute resolve* within to learn how to work *with* Me at *all* times. I can only do so to the degree that you *completely choose* a better way in your life.

In the fallen nature, which may still be present in you to some degree, your decisions at this time are more often a wish, a hope, or desire but not a real decision. A real decision is a *power* that comes from your divine nature. *Decision* means choice-power, resolve, determination, commitment, will, using your sovereign right and your God-given agency. You must completely seize your power to decide. *Agency is yours and yours alone.* I will always honor your agency and cannot be the one to choose

Chapter 11 – Respectful, Honest Conversation

for you, though I clearly share My choice and My will for you.

When you are resolute and work with Me, you will find that your ability to improve in anything and everything will definitely increase. Much good has come forth from your past level of your power of choice, but my intent is to expand your understanding of this power. It is *the* major ingredient you bring to the table to work with Me and create all the greatness that We have made covenant with the Father to bring to pass.

One of the major, godly qualities that Satan wants for you to relinquish or dilute is this *power of choice*. The weakness of choice is in fallen nature, and I want you to see how to claim this godly power of yours—an irrevocable power—and use it fully. I want you to recognize that you have not always used the fullness of this divine choice-power. I want you to choose wisely and to do so with the Light I offer to shine upon your life, to see what is before you, to create and bring greatness to pass. I want you to choose the fullness of Life that I offer to you *now*. Will it all come to pass immediately? No, but we, you and I, will begin in the most excellent manner to create in your life all the wonderful ways of our Heavenly Home and restore all the godly powers and abilities that your spirit holds now, and then actively move forward. True choice is a *decision* and a *power*, not just a possibility or hope.

Alive in Christ – *The Gift*

The pattern of fallen nature invites you to look at what is an outward, worldly reality, what has already been created and let that outward reality make the decision for you. Instead, *you* decide all the holy, righteous things you would want to create. Bring the power from *inside* of you, your innate, godly, true nature, and then let Me work with you so we can create together. You bring the power of your decision, and I will add the powers of Godly Love and Light—those two infinite elements of creation— and then nothing will stop or hinder the greatness we can create in the world, in your body, and in your life.

It is easier to see the subtle changes for good that have taken place when you look back over an expanded period of time. There are mathematical equations that show how things begin slowly and then increase exponentially. It is not just an adding on, but there is a certain power and ability that builds, increasing the divine, creative forces within you. You can accelerate that momentum by making an absolute decision and working closely with Me. There are going to be moments in your life, as you remain consistent in having Sacred Time every day with Me, in which you will experience compounding. You will have this great increase, as if an explosion, a *multiplying* effect within a short period of time. *Be patient; hang in there. This will come.*

Keep this in mind when making your decision to step up and accept fully My Gift of Life. Instead of lowering your hopes and expectations, expand them. Believe more in your godly power and true nature and My willingness to

Chapter 11 – Respectful, Honest Conversation

work with you. Do your best and I will add on. Come every day and practice working with Me. Expand with Me your keen and conscious awareness of the ability to know and love yourself, to know and love others unconditionally, to pick up on the subtle and spiritual energies, to hear the Spirit's voice and My voice letting Truth and Heaven's impressions flow through you, bringing greater wisdom and power into your life every day.

At times, you may feel that taking the time for our Sacred Time and always praying over everything may seem to take too much time and slows you down. *Hold your faith. Trust Me.* Your divine powers will build and grow exponentially, and this time spent will return great dividends.

Of all the *important* things that you can do, opening up and having Sacred Time and allowing Our Love to flow in and feel it is the beginning foundation to have a connection in which you love and feel loved. You hold open desire to receive, whether you are consciously hearing it or not, but holding faith that you *are* receiving. Your being is *hearing* Our Divine Love, Light, and Truth pouring into you and giving support for your life. From the origin of our Divine, Holy, Eternal Parents comes forth everything. I so desire to expand your connection and awareness of the Love and Light from God to you and experience how much *more* can be present in your everyday life even here on Earth.

My great desire, again, is that you read these things with prayer and an open, believing state. *Read these words out loud and listen with your whole being.* Be prayerful and read these words again and again. Be open and have a simple conversation in your unique style and from your genuine self. Be peaceful and quiet to hear in your heart more than just words, as if *the whole essence of everything that I say is a sphere of Light and Love greater than just the words.* It is delivered with My deep caring of you, My knowing you in absolute detail, My complete acceptance for you, and the complete acceptance from the Holy Father and Mother above.

Remember, the Father's judgments do not condemn. His judgment of you is a perfect awareness of every situation going on inside and outside of you. He knows exactly where you are in your eternal progression as you walk on your eternal path. His judgment of you after this segment of your life is His wise placement of where you will progress best in your eternal progression. That is the judgment of God, and it is filled with Love, which is inseparable from Truth, and Truth and Love together move you forward and give you life.

A wide band of possibilities exists of how to experience life. As you come to receive the beautiful Love that We have to offer and the Truth that is contained therein, it will be narrowed. That does not mean restricted. Instead, you will see more clearly the best way to proceed to move forward in the most exponential way. The fruits of your labors and choices will be expanded as you walk in pure alignment so that Love flows through you unrestrained at all times. You feel it. You experience it. All

Truth which holds all information that exists can flow in, bringing wisdom to your conscious mind and strength and spiritual energy into your physical being. Then you can act upon all that you righteously desire, expanding goodness while interfacing with others in peace and harmony.

My Invitation to You
My invitation to you is to better understand and feel this Divine Essence of God, Their Love and Truth which is Our Light. Be with the quiet stillness within you. Expand and multiply all good things with *gratitude*. Increase the ability to know others accurately with Our added insight. Have *all* your relationships be in a manner that is best for all concerned. Know and be clear about your true self. Feel the power and the beauty of your individuality. Claim the strength of your choice-power combined with Our wisdom. Move forward in Our Love which will nourish you and strengthen you to continue to fulfill your heart's desire in every good thing that you are about.

I desire for you to come and enjoy life to the fullest. Be Alive in Me. Be conscious, aware, and awake. *Actively live in constant joy, peace, and love.* I invite you to experience the dispersing of stress as you come to trust the Love that flows in, and experience the subtle energies from Divine to assist you to live *wisely* and *harmoniously*. Move forward empowered by a God who loves you.

My request is for you to step forward even more. Let it be that Love and Light flow in and support you, feed and nourish your spirit, and come into your physical body to strengthen it and put it into alignment with the most ideal functioning. Let Love and Light add *balance* and *variety* that you will be able to express your emotions in a beautiful manner and to fill your mind with all Truth, holy knowing, information, and awareness as you interface with the world. Let Us come forward and make this a *joyful* life for you. That is My Gift. The gift you give to Me is to receive My Gift and *be fully alive in Me.*

Chapter 12
My Atonement's Infinite Reach

My great desire is that you gain *added* understanding of the Gift of My Love which I offer to you. Additionally, I would expand your understanding of the *power* of My Atonement, that you may know how to fully receive daily improvements through My Light and through making this Atoning Gift an intricate part of your physical life and eternal being.

More Alive!
In these next chapters, I will address from different views how the Atonement might become more alive in you. I use the words *more alive* because, yes, you are alive, but there are greater levels in your ability to experience the godliness and powers of Divinity. Actively expanding your godliness comes from our Eternal Father is the *alive* of which I speak. The fullness of the Father was given to Me in My physical form. He literally was the Father of My physical body while I was here on Earth, which gave My body His exalted form. Additionally, I was given His Divine Power.

I grew in His Divine Power from childhood, and I learned and progressed in my beautiful body. I was also given the power to overcome all restrictions or forms of death. Ultimately there can be no death but only a pause and a change, a moving into new realms and dimensions as individuals progress on eternally. My desire is for you to receive life through Me as fully as I did from the Father while I was on the Earth, so that your physical body can be as if literally born of God. I will bring forth His attributes into you to clear your body of *all fallen nature.*

There are two ways to have power over death: One is to pass through the portal of death and then *quickly* reclaim the body and lift it up to life. Two is to be *immune* to a physical death altogether. Though I had the capacity to not die, I *chose* to create the ability to restore life fully from a dead body state that had held all the sins of the world. By so doing, I set this path for others who would also experience death.

I also hold within Me Heavenly Mother's powers by My perfect unity with Her. My body now holds *infinitely* the power of both Our Eternal Parents, as if this physical body had been perfectly born out of feminine Goddess and masculine God. My earthly mother, Mary, was completely filled with the holiness and Light of the Eternal Mother and Father, and she was in perfect unity and oneness with Them. I come to also give you the fullness of the Mother, if you will receive it, and being then as if you were also born of Her.

Your Ultimate Physical Body

Yea, your physical body has the perfect capacity to move forward into eternal life and even bypass death, should that be your choice. There are many different things that are offered along the way, but I speak of the *ultimate*—to be as our Eternal Mother and Father God. It is Their perfection you are heading toward. I want you to realize that when you hold such capacities and powers in your *ultimate* physical body—your perfected, immortal body—then you will have a vessel capable of receiving the fullness of the Gift of *all* My Love!

My Love is the same love that the Divine Mother and Father hold! You will have received all of eternal Truth and can know all things, for you will then be connected infinitely to *everything* that is! We have all Wisdom. We know *all* that is. This is the Gift that is given unto you— *even all that I am and all that I have.*

You have been learning from outside sources and have studied many things in this world. You have been taught by your experiences and by other individuals. You have used your mind to gather information, to reason, to figure things out, and to understand what is going on around you. You have also been prayerful. You have sought the Heavens for further Light, Truth, knowledge, understanding, power, and capacity. You have moved forward beautifully in your life.

Now is the Day for Acceleration

Now is the day for the acceleration of your personal development. This hastening is necessary and is to be greater than it has been upon the Earth heretofore. At this time the requirement for your divine advancement is different. You are asked to raise this world from its current state to one of greater glory, to be a Zion state which adheres to higher Law and Love, a Terrestrial Kingdom.

When you learn from the mind's understanding and from experiences in the world around you, you are connected to sources that can teach you many things, but not completely all. This may be in an impure state or an incomplete conclusion. I come to deliver greater Eternal Truths that can never be obtained from the mind's current capacity and by just observing and studying the world. I come to give you Truth *inseparable* from Love from the Heavenly realm. I do so that you may be taught, be instructed, and learn from this eternal source of Light, of Truth, of information, of power, and spiritual capacity. This knowledge is brought into both your spirit being *and* your physical body.

You are to learn new information from Divine Origin and from your spirit to give understanding to your mind. This learning from the greater realm is different from the way you have learned in the world. Knowledge is not just to come *from* your mind and the world, but pure Truth and information are to come *into* your mind from our Omniscient God. Yes, to understand and experience life, you will continue to learn from others around you, from the world, from experiences, and from all the beautiful information that has been discovered by using your wonderful mind and the capacities of your physical being. This physical learning adds to and works with the learning from the Eternal. How glorious it is to learn from the Source of all creation!

Two Sources for Learning
When you learn from the Heavenly realm that is within you and from the Earthly realm that is outside you, increased power comes into your learning. Your progression and your ability to absorb, to perform, to be, and to do the things that you have learned in your mind shall be greater and far beyond what you have experienced before.

I am the Mediator. I am the liaison between the *two worlds.* I am the One who becomes the Heavenly, Divine, Eternal link to your experiences of this Earth world. I am here that you may learn from *both places.* The spirit of discernment will be powerful and strong. I come to give you discernment that you might know *all* things and not take as much time to learn whether something from the outside world is absolutely true, powerful, and most beneficial for you or not. I will reveal to you if there is a greater way. You may know if the way you are choosing is the purest and the loftiest and most powerful for expediting your progression. I deeply desire to awaken your spirit to its full capacity and to have a strong interaction between your physical and spiritual self.

Your spirit and physical being are not yet infused as one. There must be complete harmony with these two aspects of your being. Your physical being must rise to the *higher* and more perfected nature that is already in your spirit. Though they reside side-by-side, they are to be brought forth and *infused as one unit,* becoming inseparable. Before this infusion can take place, there must be the *complete* harmonious agreement and alignment with Divine way. In order for this to take place, I must teach you in a spiritual manner more Truth, which must also be in complete balance and harmony with God's Eternal Love.

Bring the Two Worlds into Unity
Perhaps in prayer, meditation, or a vision, you have gone into a beautiful spiritual state, energetically entering into a realm or dimension where you perceive and understand things of a spiritual nature. This is wonderful and good, for you have begun to create something spiritually that can have an influence and manifest in the outward physical world. This spiritual understanding can help you to also see the Truth that is on Earth as it connects with the Truth in Heaven. This helps *bring the two worlds into unity*. This is part of rescuing the world from its fallen nature. The reclaiming from the invasion of Satan is part of the mission that has been given to you.

When you are connected and empowered by your knowing from a spiritual space, the Truth in your spirit and the Truth in your physical world match. Your whole being resonates and says: *This is true!* The concept you learned from the world, which is Truth, now has an added vibration of power and will support you in being able to live the Truth and know how to apply it in life.

The Truth that exists in your spirit is a replica of the higher ways of Heaven. The uniting of these *matching* Truths will awaken your being and empower you to live in alignment with the Truth even more than you could with just the belief you have previously learned from the world. *There is a power that comes from your spiritual side that will give life to the physical.* There is also the reality and the power of the physical world that will add dimension to your spiritual understanding. This union of views and beliefs also supports the unifying of your spirit and your physical being.

They are both needed. One is not greater or superior in any manner than the other. They are both highly, vitally necessary for your eternal progression. You are here to understand the application, the presentation, the power of spirituality, and of spiritual concepts and spiritual energies manifested in physical form. *Your body is a physical manifestation of spiritual Truth and is literally a formation of Truth.* You are to enjoy this physical body. You are to enjoy this physical world. You are to understand how to work with a variety of physical matter and with people on all levels.

I Am Asking You to Be Vulnerable
The first step in accomplishing this union of Truth is for you to be willing to receive from the spiritual realm. Often the mind, in its fallen nature pattern, will cling to the

opinions already present and, without recognizing this tendency, will close off from new understanding. It is a manifestation of your unwillingness to recognize error or limits in what you already know. You must have the spirit of *humility*. When I say to be '*open*', or when I ask you to '*open up*', *I am asking you to be vulnerable*. I am asking you to be willing to recognize the possibility of your error of thought and understanding. Being '*open*' means you are ready to receive more than what you have, and not just to know, but to *be* and *live* the Truth you receive. Be as a little child who is open and willing to learn anew.

Let Me Become Your Prophet
I ask you to exercise your faith and believe that spiritual inspiration and Truth can come to you. I truly desire to give to you greater understanding from Heaven through your spirit and into your physical being. This understanding will create a greater expansion of righteousness in your life. What you receive from Me will also be an enlightenment for times to come. This can only come by *new and expanded revelations to you*.

These new personal revelations and witnessing will be added to what you have learned from the world and will reveal a power to live the Truth you know or to correct any falsehood or limited understanding. Turn no more just to the good teachings of great men and to the prophets alone. Turn to Me. I will reveal to you. *That's when I become your prophet.* Then, with Me, *you* also will be-

Chapter 12 – My Atonement's Infinite Reach

come the prophet and receive personal revelation for your own life. No one will stand between you and Me.

Your conscious mind will then understand it is a powerful and vital part of you, a necessary instrument to bring Heaven and Earth together. Yes, I want you to consciously understand all things. More than just consciously understanding, let your understanding go beyond its present limitations. When your mind becomes pure and exact, it will witness the expansion of truth that has been learned on Earth. You will then link to the *spiritual Truth* that is already within you! This Truth is now expanded, added upon, and empowered. Truth will become on Earth as it is in Heaven.

I want the truth on this earth and the Truth of Heaven to come together. Work with Me. Let Me pour the Holy Truth of all things into you. I will teach you all things as they are in the Heavens and show you that this same knowledge is also on this Earth. Again, I can teach you *any* Truth that you can learn from this world. I will teach you in the holiest of manner.

In your physical world, there may be an understanding, a pattern, or a belief that is contrary or not completely in harmony with something that you believe. So I ask you to come unto Me that I might reveal the Truth unto you. I will replace your false understanding or increase your knowledge so that Truth becomes spiritual food. You will be able to completely implement this into your life until Truth becomes a full part of you. Let Truth, delivered to your being from Divine, become your way of life in this physical world.

Coming to Oneness

A testimony of the heart is different than the testimony of the mind. Gaining a testimony of the heart strengthens and expands the testimony of the mind. The Holy Spirit will bear witness to your mind when something is true. There is also an additional witness that is born through the feelings and knowing of the heart. You will not just *know* the fact to be eternally true, but you will *love* the Truth and *desire* to be one with such Divine ways.

You are also to have a witness to your whole being. Your body's intelligences can hold and be united with Truth. You quietly and powerfully know the truth within you. There is a part of you that says: *This is so! This is Truth!* You might not even consciously understand what Truth stirs within you when the light of truth is first delivered, but there is a draw, there is a feeling of energy from your spiritual self that is moving you forward. Inwardly you desire something very keenly, something that is preparing you to rise up greater in righteousness.

It is one thing to know of a wonderful concept, but another thing to make it a working reality in your life. Let's talk about applying Truth to your relationships. You find it difficult to bring forth a *constant* state of love, joy, peace, and harmony into a relationship. You simply do not know what else to do to create the harmony you seek, having done all you can think of. This limit of ideas

Chapter 12 – My Atonement's Infinite Reach

is because you are only working from logic, the reasoning of your mind, and the teachings from the world. You need the spiritual knowing to give life and expansion to not only what to do, but also the power to bring harmony into the relationship.

Your God-Given Birthright

The expansion of learning and being empowered from the spiritual realm can apply to any situation in your life. Think about your physical body. Everyone desires to be healthy, strong, and full of vitality. *It is your God-given birthright to have great strength and radiating health, but you alone cannot manifest this in your body—not to the degree of its potential.* Because of fallen nature, there is interference in your physical body that prevents it from being at its peak of perfection. This is true for everyone, even those who at the beginning seem to be exceptionally healthy.

I tell you that there is *something* in the physical body's capacity and pattern that is *incorrect* or *incomplete*. From the beginning of each person's life on Earth, there is a defiant, destructive energy that is in total opposition and has destroyed the body's original design as it was before the Fall. *The body's true nature and design holds continual, natural improvement.* We are to restore the full power of the body's ability to advance in capacity, strength, and vital health where there is no limit to its progressing into *eternalness*. How exciting is that, my dear friend?

Come unto Me that I may teach you! I will reveal to you and create with you a higher and better way in your body. I am the One to expand your understanding through your sincere prayers and your righteous decisions. I will grant unto you greater knowledge about your body *portion by portion*. I say *portion by portion* because you learn best in this world in segments that fit together in sequence. With the power of vibration I will give you the first thing you must know. When you have applied that information and are ready to receive more I will give a second portion, then a third, and so on. In time you will have a complete understanding of what is needed to move your health forward. You will also have manifested the reality of Truth and Love's full effect upon your physical body.

Open Up Your Eyes
I will be glad to *open up your eyes* when you truly desire to see that which you do not yet see: to see the Truth, to see any error in understanding, patterns, or behaviors. Everyone has a blind spot at the beginning. Everyone has a place where they do not hear what is really being said. As a result, an idea comes through in a muffled manner and is rearranged so that your comprehension is converted into a *misunderstanding.*

Walking a holy walk yourself is not possible because of the *erroneous* teachings and *false* conclusions of truth presented in this world. However, when you come with sincerity and are steadfast in your desire, I will impart to you the Truth in its purer presentation. My desire is to

Chapter 12 – My Atonement's Infinite Reach

open up the Truth in your life, even the *living Truth*, which is Truth coupled with Divine Light. Living Truth then has the power to become a reality in every moment of your life. Another way I could say this is: *The most powerful way to know Truth, through the greater imparting of My Atoning Gift I have for you, is by our communication and our time together.* Come in mighty prayer unto your Father in Heaven. Be with Us; I am One with Him. I am at your side as your liaison. I will pray *with* you.

So I stand here ready to deliver your heart's desire and to return unto you the reply from your Father in Heaven. *I am the One to transfer everything to you.* Yes, oft times it also goes through the Holy Spirit, who comes to reside with you when you seek for Truth and Light. As you are in constant sincerity of seeking the Holy Spirit—also called the Holy Ghost—He will reside with you, illuminating your consciousness and your conscience. I am the One who comes unto you, with the support of the Holy Spirit, to bring the two worlds of Heaven and Earth together.

A Living Testimony

You have received a testimony. But what does that mean? The moment you hear or study something, there can be an illumination of your being that testifies: *This is Truth!* You know it. In that moment it is strong with you. This is the witnessing to the mind, confirming that it is true. Next, there is to be the testimony of the heart. To mature and fulfill the purpose of a testimony of the mind and heart, *an additional step is needed.* Pray for the spiritual Light of Truth to interface, witness, and give a testimony to your whole being. Your entire body will know: *This is true!* This complete witness and testimony are needed to move forward with full power and become the testified truth.

Now the testimony will be stronger and be sustained to influence your life. Even then, constant nourishment to this testimony is needed to hold *a living testimony*—one that is witnessing to you continually, providing you this constant nourishment and manifesting the power of the Truth in your life.

Sometimes you might think; *Well, I have received a testimony of this*, and you stop there. Oh, My dear precious one, please, please, recognize this is just a beautiful beginning, an opening to more. Continue to pray that your spiritual knowing of the Truth expands in you and becomes part of you constantly. The Heavens will continue to witness the Truth unto you. My power shall keep this Truth alive and active in you. Then it becomes a *constant burning* within you, just as it was when the witness was first received. Now, with an active testimony, the Truth will grow.

Once the physical being, which includes the mental body (*testimony to the mind*), the emotional body (*testimony of the heart*) and physical (*testimony to the whole being*), has received this spiritual witnessing, your whole physical being can now align with the testimony that is already in your spirit being. Now this glorious Truth will

Chapter 12 – My Atonement's Infinite Reach

become part of your life, naturally and easily flowing forth with increasing improvements.

You may ask: *Can I receive a testimony to the whole being at one moment? Can we take this through all the levels immediately?* Sometimes yes, but not always. I may start with a testimony of the mind, but there may be some beliefs and patterns in you that are in opposition or are not congruent with the new belief. You will need to recognize this and be willing to *let go of the old.* Seek to have Me assist in removing this false way, for it will block further testimony. Then you will be ready to receive the added witnessing and have a living testimony.

Alive in Christ – *The Gift*

Chapter 13
Making Truth Permanent

Even with a testimony, continue to seek for greater Truth. Truth must grow, becoming stronger and taking root within you. *Truth and Love are to unify your spirit and your physical being.* Let holy Light continue to witness and nourish the Truth. Then you are empowered, and you continue to manifest this Light in your life. There is a certain portion of linear time in this world that is necessary to fulfill each part of your progression. When you exercise yourself in bringing a *spiritual* infusion of Heaven's Light and Truth into your *physical* being, you begin to grow your own Tree of Life with its delicious fruits and strong roots to remain with you forever.

Now you have a greater capacity to unite Truth learned from both sides of your being, *physical and spiritual.* Momentum will take hold. Let's use an analogy: A young man desires to learn to farm. In his first year, he will learn many things. After he has farmed for many years, he will become more productive. He will know how to move things forward, to create the most ideal conditions for his plants to grow at their optimum, *and* to do so in the most rapid manner. At the same time, the plants are receiving the most wholesome and pure nutrition so that they are good, solid, healthy and filled with vitality. This progress is the same for you as you are learning.

You could work upon many things at one time, but *sometimes there is value in taking just one concept, one Truth until it has taken root in you and is with constant testimony.* This living Truth within you will strengthen other Truths that you have learned. You will build momentum, accelerating your spiritual progression. By contrast, the pattern in the world keeps you flitting from one commandment and righteous way of living to another. If you focus on this unstable pattern, it can prevent newly learned righteousness from taking root and strengthening in you.

The fruits of our efforts working together manifest in how you now feel, think, and behave. You will find yourself thinking: *This Truth is very much part of my nature now. This holy way of being is easy for me to do. It flows forth naturally from me. These qualities are with me at all times. This Truth is part of me, even inseparable from me.* If you do not yet feel that your testimony is powerful and constant, and you are still struggling with it, then come to Me. I will reveal to you what *virtue* needs to be strengthened to support the truth you have received.

As you seek for principles of Truth, *also* seek to be one with the holy virtues of Love that accompany the principles. The holy virtues are necessary and balancing to principles just as justice and mercy complement and balance each other. All principles of truth are kept strong and growing with the virtues. Work with Me to strengthen a needed virtue to be a strong part of your life. Then keep working with Me to make the corresponding principle to be a part of your being. There is great value in making a mighty change in one area of your life because that change will influence all aspects of your being.

All Truth Is Connected
All Truth is connected. When you emphasize one principle, it will strengthen all other principles in you. So, just focus on one virtue you want to improve and stay with that even though it seems life is constantly bringing you many different challenges, and you feel: *Well, I need to go learn that now.* Do not jump from one idea to another, or *nothing* will be accomplished and brought to *excellence.* Yes, you are to bring all holy ways and Truth to be part of you. There is much to learn and become, but hold to one thing that it may be constant with you. I will work with you and teach you well how to be a good planter and to bring forth good fruit until you have an abundant harvest and strong, healthy fruit. So let us begin with just one, *one* truth that you specialize in.

There are a wide variety of choices. Contemplate and really think: *What attributes, what quality, or what truth do I desire to have in my life that would really make my feel like I have moved forward? What do the results look like for me? When would I feel that it would be complete? What is the thing that I desire?* Take time to be prayerful, and I will guide you.

I am so desirous to give you the fullness of everything. Begin with Me that I might give you the portion you are ready for. I will lead you into the whole. Commit with sincerity and devotion in daily prayer, asking for the constant nourishment of Light and of a greater clarity of understanding for your choice in improvement. Let your emotions and thoughts begin to stir your desire and prepare you to make changes within. Continue to build no matter how long it takes and do so always with *Me*.

How Long Will It Take?
The length of time does not matter. Perhaps you select something that is going to take years. You could easily say: *I would become discouraged if that were the case.* You may want to choose something to focus on that is not quite so intense for you. Yet, if this bigger project is a great desire, then stay with it. The large improvement that you have chosen to make will also have a broader influence on your life.

Let's say you determine to stay with a longer undertaking—a large one which encompasses many other things—so that even though you may move forward on one focus, you will draw into you also many other powerful changes that are naturally going to take place as well. For example, let us measure the degree of effect it would have on your life. Take an arbitrary number of 1000. That is a large number because your goal is going to take years to accomplish. By implementing this quality, however, you will draw to you many other great qualities and Truths attached to your mission—because it is quite significant—a major undertaking in your life.

Let's say you choose something else that is *not* as big and has a value of 10 on the complexity and difficulty scale, and you only need to stay focused for a short period of time to make the change. You accomplish your goal which has brought very powerful changes within that you definitely notice: *This feels deep within me! It feels part of me! I have made amazing changes in My life!* Though your endeavor was not major, you have experienced a very definite result and have acknowledged in that time period that the quality or virtue has become part of you. As you continue with a focused strategy, you will find that when you 'plant again', it will take less time. Even though you may pick a bigger topic which could take more time, it will move forward much more rapidly because you have stayed with a certain improvement before and brought it to completion. *You have made it part of your nature.*

Making It Part of Your Nature

Making something a habit is not the same as *making it part of your nature*. A habit can be broken. Your *nature* stays with you no matter what. Regardless of what conditions come along, you remain who you are. When it is your nature to be honest, you stay honest, notwithstanding the outward circumstance. When it is your nature to take good care of your body and eat well, then you will always find a way to make that happen. When patience is your virtue, and you have no fallen nature in you, no matter what happens, you are patient. When you first accept and believe an idea to be true and receive a testimony of such, you have begun the first step in making this part of your nature.

Next, you must set an *intention* to make this part of your life. Many do not realize that *getting a testimony* is not the same thing as believing in something. Following your decision to become this greater way involves *practicing the application*. You will grow in the understanding of the Truth and expand and improve your capacity. With repeated practice and application, it can become a *habit*, and you may move forward with a behavior and do very well for a period of time. Then some circumstance comes along, and it throws you off. For example, you may have been very patient, but when an extra challenging circumstance comes along, impatience resurfaces. What I say is the new way may have become a habit, a very good habit and may be with you *most* of the time. It may be strong, but that does not mean it is your nature completely.

To make your new way of being *fully* your nature, all fallen nature patterns and beliefs must be *completely* removed. Also, you must absolutely *love* the concept or way of being. Loving something to that point may take time. Sometimes when you start something new, it might not be comfortable, and you might not like doing or being this way. But by staying with your goal until it becomes a reality and an eternal way, you will go beyond the difficulty, and it will become *delightful* and *enjoyable* to you. When I work with you in making an improvement

Chapter 13 – Making Truth Permanent

in your life, I will always provide the Love and Light to attend and assist you in learning to love and embrace the Holy Way. Then I can bless you to make this new way a part of your nature.

Oh, how I desire to work with you! *This is what the Gift of My Atonement is all about.* Make a decision for an improvement, one that is to be more than a habit; decide to make it a *part of your eternal nature.* What divine quality and way of living do you want as a great strength in your life? Stop and ponder what you would like to change. Prepare yourself so you and I can set firmly the task to bring a new principle of Truth in great strength to be *one* with your physical nature. Have your prayer right now and decide with Me. Get a testimony of the improvement or change you desire. *For the moment, stop reading.* Pray. Decide. Let Me strengthen your choice.

Now that you have prayerfully made your decision and resolve, the power to create is set into motion. Get clear in your physical mind. Hold the thought and visualize until your body resonates with it. Ask Me, and I will work with you to bring the *spirit* and *energy* of the chosen Truth into your spirit and your body. Your spirit being will quickly receive My infusion of Light, set with a specific purpose. The divine power and energy will grow as you continue working with Me, praying and holding firm to your decision. I will continue with you until the whole of the eternal quality is infused into every aspect of your being, and is *permanently, inseparably, and forevermore* part of you!

Your Spirits Vital Desire

Working with Me is actually something you learn to do in *degrees*. Your desires for change and improvement will be expedited smoothly and rapidly as you learn to work with Me. Then I will infuse the two aspects—*spiritual and physical*—into one. Working with Me in this manner is the vital foundation. I so desire to give to you in such a manner that Truth and God's Divine Nature become part of you in this physical body. *I so desire for this to be.*

What I know is that *you also* desire it. That desire is present more in some than others and in different degrees of exposure. I am telling you, your pure spirit desires the previously made choices in Heaven, which are greater than you are experiencing at the moment. I would that you and I awaken this passion physically! This fire! This desire! Physically make this choice that *your spirit* has already made.

You made the choice to come to Earth in its *fallen state* and to fully experience bringing spiritual truth into physical form. Your exaltation and the complete overcoming of fallen nature can only be accomplished with Me. There are so many different ways to go about this. I have given you a simple way to prayerfully make a decision about one main principle or quality that you would like to powerfully create in your life. Keep this your focus until it becomes part of your nature.

How you will choose to work through your salvation with Me is completely up to you. The world at large is far too

Chapter 13 – Making Truth Permanent

casual and delays this vital mission of life here on earth. Even those who profess My name also tend to approach this mission casually. I am asking you, though, to get serious and *hasten* your repentance and personal transformation with Me *now*.

Once a quality becomes embedded in you, *and I have sealed the Truth in your nature*, no one or no circumstance can then change that. Continue on to bring eternal ways into this physical body of yours, so that you might embrace the *fullness* of what I have to give to you. *This fullness is the transformation of your body being born anew, as if it had been born out of God the Father and Mother.* Continue diligently with Me until I transform *all* of your physical being into its true nature. Let's make the change become a complete, permanent part of you *never to reverse*. No power, no outside source can ever remove this way from your being! My changes in you are meant to be eternal.

Then Nothing Can Take Your Life!
In reality, nothing could have taken My life. I gave My life that I might prepare the path for *others* to follow. No force or person caused My death, or the separation of My Spirit and physical body. I *chose* to go through that separation. You have been given that same gift. You have the ability to receive the fullness of life and Divine Nature as you receive the fullness of the Mother and the Father that I hold in Me. You may receive all Eternal Truth and Love from your spiritual side and infuse it into your physical side, making Divine Nature your nature until life

is as much with you as it is with Me. *Then nothing can take your life!*

I want your mind to be *expanded*. I would like you to take the various thoughts that I have given to you and ask for a testimony. Ask that there be a continual feeding of the spirit of Truth to come through your *spiritual side* into your *physical side,* creating a full living testimony fed by continual Light from Heaven. Let that testimony, that knowing, become so much a part of you and of your nature, that no *one*, nor any *circumstance,* can take this Divine Way out of you. You will not only know Truth, and have a testimony of Truth, but you will also be that Truth.

Even now you might ask: *Could this really be so permanent in my being that I do not falter?* I say to you, yes. I am teaching you that it is not an absolute for you to experience death. The world certainly does not believe such, but I am teaching this to you. *These are the same teachings I gave to Enoch, who did not experience death*. I will teach more in this book about the variety of ways one conquers death.

I am speaking to you through written word. Come and gain a testimony of eternal life, even in this world. Then let Us nurture this witness. Let Us nurture the idea that *I am so with you every step of the way,* that Divine Nature can be brought forth and made your nature. Believe that you will become eternal in your physical body. Take one quality, one way, one Truth, or one behavior, enhanced and blessed by the spiritual and the physical energy. *Then we begin the delivery of Eternal Life from My Atonement.* I will unite your spirit and your physical body together. Though they currently reside side-by-side, yet they are to be brought forth into complete oneness. Eternally inseparable!

You must *choose* for this union to be, and then *hold* to that choice. Select whatever righteousness you greatly believe in and desire to have in your life, and, then let you and I create this *together*. Remain true and faithful until the victory is complete in you. *It will be.* So again, I am asking—I am asking you in many ways—that you trust even more, and understand even more until your faith is a knowing, never wavering, but constant as if all has already been completed. Begin now with a full intent, and be steadfast and diligent. Create with Me the greatest gift you can give your Eternal Parents: *your perfected, exalted self.*

Know Me—Know Truth
Let Me give you Eternal Life. Let Me create this with you. I cannot do it alone without you, and you cannot do it alone without Me. *Yet, together We can.* Let Us do away with everything that is not eternal way. Let Us clear you and make you pure that you might see all things, believe all things, hope all things, establish all things, create all things, and hold within you the eternal pattern, even the *Gift of God*. The Gift of God is the gift of Their Eternal Life. This I will deliver to you so it will be as if you also had been born of God. Then you are truly heirs in *fullness*.

Come and know Me, and let Me come and work with you. Be ye steadfast and have no concern for the time that it will take. Only have concern that you are committed and that the commitment *grows* within you so that We are daily moving forward together. It will be powerful in your life.

What I am teaching is a foundation for all that you are yet to receive. Take what I have said and be prayerful about it. Take the time that you might read again these words until they are strong in you. Oh, I would invite you to come and read this again until you take hold, and the Truth of what I have presented shines brightly within you. Be in gratitude so you are prepared to receive further. *I will be here with you.* I am your liaison between Heaven and Earth to bring all of your heart's righteous desires into physical reality.

The very fact that you are on Earth at this time and that you are reading this message at this very moment is a witness to you of your spiritual development heretofore and of your readiness to step into an amplified application of My Atonement. You are ready to implement a glorifying of your Holy Mother and Father by receiving all Their Love, all Their Eternal Truth, and all Their Glory. This fullness of Their Light is what I am offering you. *This is the fullness of My Gift.* I am showing you the one way, yea, through Me, that you may accomplish complete removal of *all* fallen nature and experience your exaltation! Oh, how this will bring such joy to our Eternal Gods, our Eternal Parents!

I am He who is the Christ. I am He who comes to deliver your exaltation, your eternal life, your oneness with the Heavenly Mother and Eternal Father. I am He who brings the fullness of all that into this physical world that you might shine brightly and give back the glory of your exaltation unto Them. Precious is the holy Love and the Light They give to you. Be one with Me, and I will be one with you, as we move forward together in the Glory of our Holy Parents. My precious friend, know that *I am with you and always will be.*

Chapter 14
A New Way

I am extremely mindful of everything going on. I am extremely aware of the frustrations, the steps forward or backward, the awareness and lack of awareness, and all that is going on in *your* life. The idea that God knows all is not new to you. You have been taught, for the most part, that God knows *everything*. The real application of this reality is not fully recognized as to how God's omnipotence and omniscient applies to *your* life. Neither is there a true understanding of the power of God, let alone a comprehension of God Himself.

You go about your days with many activities taking place in each moment—all that is a concern to you—with thoughts that are here and there and everywhere. Throughout your day you are unaware of My awareness of you, nor are you aware of the Father, the Heavens and all those that come to work with you. In reality, you are often attended by many spiritual beings who come to assist you in every possible manner. You don't know it, but many are there to guide, direct and support you when you are ready for that support. We do not interfere, but we do support and in wisdom, we guide, prompt, inspire, add Light, and give our Love.

Becoming Aware

Becoming aware is a necessity as you go about your daily life. You can do so by knowing that I am present. I am aware of what is taking place and am mindful of the greatest and tiniest of details. I am right there present beside you for *My spirit is with you always;* My spirit's presence is the same as if I were there personally in the *fullness* of My being. I'm there for the purpose of pouring Light into you. I am there to support you in what is going on, though I never interfere. I will insert when you are open to My input. When you are ready to have added Light, allow Me to enhance your own wisdom by bringing forth a greater capacity from your own spirit, a new thought or inspired thought added to yours.

We offer this Light and support *openly and freely.* Yet it is not fully used. It is taught but not understood. I cannot emphasize enough the great honor the Father and I hold for you, the mindfulness We have of the most minute detail and how supportive and how connected We are with *you.*

In this fallen nature world there are many different ways to relate to others. On one hand, people may feel distant, disconnected, and unsupported by others—*alone.* On the other hand, people may feel that others are too close, interfering rather than being supportive. When someone tries to interfere or control another person's life, the response may be to push away. However, some may yield, letting another make all the decisions. Often people try to control by thinking they are helping or doing 'what must be done', basing their actions on their own interpretation of what the scriptures and commandments say. All these varieties of interactions can end up causing tension and relationship problems. If you have control or abandonment issues, it is easy to transfer those issues into a belief that God is also controlling or absent.

God's commandments are often misunderstood. You might see them as interference. The commandments may feel like a heavy burden, something trying to control you, something you must be obedient to 'or else'. You insert all sorts of consequences, and the result is feeling alienated, shameful, sinful, and a failure, including other negative responses. *The commandments are not harsh demands.* They are inspired directions to support you, not to control you or to interfere. Commandments are an invitation to come and create with God. They are given in kindness to say: *Following this direction is a way that will support you in your life and bring you freedom, joy, peace, and love.*

God, the Father, knows you. You are His child. In your Eternal progression you are quite advanced, but relative to God, Our Father, *you are still a child*. The sacred, holy, beautiful blessing to know you has been given to Me by the Father. That is what the Atonement afforded Me. I am One with the mind of God who knows you in perfection. He knows every pattern you have ever developed and exactly how you will choose to respond. The connection is not a control; it is perfect awareness and knowing you very well.

Life is meant to have a variety of choices. With the Father I create *energetic variances* in your life, giving you different possibilities to choose from. I know your abilities, what will or will not influence you, and what your choices will be under certain conditions. We hold the doors open to all things so that there is no power from the Heavens, no power from even God, the Father, the Eternal One, to corral and *force* you into any one place. Your life really is a series of results from what you have created and what you will create. I am not saying others do not also create a variety of conditions; everyone contributes. I am saying that God is not controlling everything in your life. His hand and powers are here to support you and, at the same time, I will bring to pass the intentions I have for the world.

Finding True Guidance
The support and the guidance are a plea for you to come to an awareness of the closeness with Us and the *safety* of that closeness. Some see God as close and interfering while others see Him as distant, far away, and uncaring. Some feel God is controlling while others feel He has abandoned everyone on the Earth to let happen what will. I would that you come to know and experience the Love the Father and I have for you. Then you will understand the perfect majesty of interaction and involvement We have with you and the world.

Chapter 14 – A New Way

The truth is the Father's Light always, always, *always* pours into you, never-ending. In the busyness of daily activities and challenges, you are not aware of how close and present We are in your life. When someone stands next to you, even though at that moment you were not directly thinking about that person, you are *indirectly* conscious of a presence. I would invite you to feel and to know Our presence with you in the same way. So expand your thinking to realize and ponder what I have said about how aware and close in spirit We constantly are to you and always there to support you.

Perhaps you have had moments when you have called out but felt God was not there; He did not seem to answer. Some, when they pray and request, hold the belief that their prayer will not be answered. They have closed themselves off to His desired support. If such is the situation with you, ask to have Me help you let go of that feeling, that belief, or that pattern which says that God is not there for you. The truth is *He is with you. I am with you.*

My emphasis is for you to recognize how supportive, how close, how aware, how loving, and desirous We all are to be there for you—not to take over your choice, not to do everything for you, but to support you in your choices. When you desire enlightenment to make a choice that is most pure to your spirit's desire and in line with holy ways, you are prepared to receive the Light from Us. We will illuminate your being so that from within you can be aware of different possibilities for moving forward righteously.

For example, when you are having a 'heated' conversation, you will most likely act on the patterns of yesterday. In that moment you *could* be given different ways of responding and different things you could say. If you have chosen the lesser of possibilities, your personal Light dims, your choices diminish, and you stay in patterns of yesterday, which are not necessarily your most joyful for the moment. Remember, *We are here to empower you to your highest way by being fully aware of other people and the circumstances around you.*

The Down Side to Habits
The fact that your body can establish habits is great. Having an automatic response is helpful and valuable, but auto-responses can also interfere if you respond from old, lesser patterns from the past. I am moving you forward to the Zion state which is a higher way of living. In this greater realm of Light, I invite you to *not* act out of habit. The ideal way is to act in each instance from your illuminated spirit's inspired responses, so in each moment you can have greater Light, seeing all possibilities and choosing carefully what will serve all best. I desire the *optimum* response from you by your continually receiving My Light, bringing you new thoughts.

Habits have served you well; however, they have been created under the influence of the *fallen nature.* You have some habits that are not necessarily the most honorable, and yet these habits are leading your life. Even your 'good' habits are only the best of this world. I desire to create a new world, a Zion order, which is much different and at a higher level of Light, Love, and Law. I am inviting you to step forward out of the pattern of habits and replace them with inspired thoughts, *new for each moment*, a refreshed newness of Light-based decisions, received from the Light of Eternal Mother and Father. Because you are created out of this beautiful essence of God, Their Light is in you and can give you in-the-moment wisdom and divine capacity to act in the highest way in every moment.

A New Way

The new way is for you to be *constantly* aware of how close We are and *always* allow Us to pour in Divine Light to illuminate your spirit with a knowing that enables you to be *much more aware* of *all* things going on around you. Your decision is then made with the unification of God's empowering Light, which your spirit and your physical being desire. *You can then move forward to make your choices with improvement every day.* So today you can make wiser choices than yesterday, even if it is just a small improvement. This is good. You can move forward with significant changes. The more you allow the awareness of this fresh new way of being, the more you will come to know that We are ready to work with you and to feel that you can turn at any moment and speak to Us. *It does not need to be a formal prayer.* All holy thoughts, all sincere thoughts, and communication sent unto Us in whatever way you may present are prayers.

We invite you to allow Our Light to illuminate you to the *maximum* capacity that can be yours for each day. Let each day be fresh and new and different with Us. When you have this open connection to Us during the day, and you have your prayers and your Sacred Time with Us, then throughout the night the holy truths will continue to illuminate greater understanding and enhance your capacities. So, while you are not working on improvements, you are still improving.

Old energy patterns diminish when you add Our Light's power to your spirit's capacity. Often you become frustrated by old patterns; you feel locked into them. I am going to say this very clearly: *You are not locked into them.* Very often the world holds the belief that your patterns and your habits keep you stuck because they are greater than you are. They are only *energy patterns* in your physical body, and, though very powerful, are *surmountable*. When you truly desire to move forward to a different and better way, increased power comes when My Light is added. The once binding and controlling patterns dissipate completely, and the negative is overcome. Now your eternal progression allows you to move forward each moment in a beautiful, up-scaled way every day.

Embrace New Patterns
You and I both recognize a pull to the old, familiar way that may still be tempting you to choose the lesser. But with *practice,* you may become very good at being able to quickly shift an old pattern and create a new. Keep in mind that I said your capacity to overcome a negative and embrace a better ideal way *when you work with Me*

in this New Way will come to be so powerful in you that your transitions, in time, will be very quick and eventually can take place *in the moment of decision*.

Let's consider a behavior pattern or an addiction you have decided to overcome, and you have begun exercising with Me in applying an ample, fresh newness of Divine Light. You are accepting and embracing the New Way until you have a *testimony that your negative pattern or addiction can be overcome*. More important than changing the pattern is *changing your belief* that the pattern *can* be changed. Now you faithfully exercise yourself in the testimony of truth, with God's power and Me working with you, along with your *spirit's power that has the capacity to be greater than any habit*. You act and become stronger. You have had a little improvement. Your behavior has not changed quite as much as you want, and there is still a little bit of a pull to the old way. But you have begun. Just keep praying, working with Me and keep making your efforts. Ah, dear one, that is so important!

Fallen nature locks your behaviors, patterns, addictions, and unfavorable responses into your physical structure. When a belief is set repeatedly into your conscious mind, then the fallen nature energy of the world stops you from breaking this pattern, and *your thoughts bind you*. Your psychological belief is stronger than your physiological response. Recognize that when you work with Me, your Divinity is stronger than anything that is set in the physical body. The physical body will respond as you direct it to respond. This physical form is *very trainable* and will learn to respond to your teaching.

Five Significant Aspects
There are five significant aspects to change that make what I am saying different from the attempts you have made before. First, your *decision is* a firm resolve, the ability to use this *choice-power from your spirit,* which is a godly power. Your current ability to choose from your physical being has the weakness of *fallen nature* that contains the energy of doubt, powerlessness, and disbelief to weaken, divert, or destroy your intent. One more time, the New Way is that you decide with your spirit and My Light, not with your mortal mind alone.

The se*cond* part to add to the first is *to take this decision to testimony*, a spiritual witness, and a reinforcement of your decision. If you still doubt you have the faith necessary, then begin by praying for faith, which comes from God in the first place. This step of gaining a testimony must be fervently prayed for every day until you feel a change in your belief, until you really do feel the knowing that: *I can do this! This can be a reality.* Your spirit wants the new way. Your physical being also truly wants the new way.

Third, you are *working with Me* and using an ample increased amount of Divine Light, greater than you normally have had on a daily basis in the past. Remember, there is always a certain amount of this 'fuel' and power that is delivered and present with you each day; howev-

Chapter 14 – A New Way

er, I am now delivering a greater portion to specifically create a new way in you. You and I have taken on the project together. The old way was, at best, to pray for help and then continue working on the problem by yourself, using only the abilities of the physical being, and you were not aware of working side by side with Me in each moment.

Another inferior way is to pray and then leave it all up to Me. I remind you, *I will not do for you the portion you can do yourself.* This is for your ability to grow and advance. I already have the ability to convert negative energy and patterns into positive *living truth*. Now it's yours to also learn how to make changes and become strong. I'm here to add the extra power you do not yet have.

This is a *together* project. You are to exercise all your capacities from both your spirit and your physical being, and I am adding to yours all that is needed to complete the task. The idea of spiritually visualizing and creating has gained attention and is used in the world. However, the ingredient that is missed is doing so with *Me*. People may draw the energy from the world and the 'energy of the universe,' but they do not include the Master of the Universe and thus receive significantly lesser results which often do not remain.

The *fourth* is *focusing on one divinely inspired, greatly desired improvement* or change to act as a catalyst for all other changes to take place and *developing the capacity* in your physical body to do so. Exercise with Me by cre-

171

ating and recreating with both aspects of your being, spiritual and physical. First, spiritually create what you want, and then practice in reality. An analogy is that if you were to pick up one part of a tablecloth and keep lifting, the whole table cloth will eventually be picked up. *All Truth is connected and is really one Truth.*

Fifth is gratitude, the multiplier. Express gratitude to God by being grateful for what is good at the moment while also praying for the increase to be better. *Daily expressing thanks will greatly accelerate the improvements.* Being unhappy and focusing on what is not yet created only takes away your power to create and directs your Light to reinforce the very negative you are desiring to overcome. Gratitude also leads to joy, and joy stands right alongside gratitude as a powerful component to making mighty changes and transitions to your True Divine Nature.

Spirit of Victory

Once the ability to overcome and create anew is set into your physical being, and you and I together have the spirit of victory present, the momentum will build until your ability to overcome any fallen nature pattern will be rapid.

You had a spirit life before coming to Earth and are an advanced child of God. Your future is to be in the likeness of your Eternal Heavenly Parents. I would that you are free to progress and to be empowered to live as you desire. I know that your desires are beautiful, and you look

Chapter 14 – A New Way

forward to greater ways of being. You desire to be more loving, more patient, more thankful, more joyful, and more successful in every righteous way of life. *A quiet knowing of your greater self exists within you.*

Always there is a moving forward. Sometimes you are not pleased with where you are, so you think: *Well. Today I have moved forward only a slight step from yesterday, if even that!* Yes, the journey before you is long, and the journey behind you was long. It is called Eternity, *and* it is to be joyful. You are to be in joy with what, where, and who you are. This is so vitally important for you. Our Heavenly Parents are constant Peace, Love, and Joy. This is your True Nature also. Join with Me to bring your True Nature completely into your physical life. I will expedite our journey and make your travel swifter, and help you gain momentum along this long and wonderful course.

Alive in Christ – *The Gift*

Chapter 15
Developing the Zion Way

I have made some mention of Zion. This is the new world I am creating with you in preparation for My return. This is the Terrestrial Glory—the second level of the Kingdom of Light that will be here during My Millennial reign on Earth—as I shall surely come again to this Earth. I will not come to the world in its fallen state again. All who abide there will have conquered fallen nature. *You have been prepared before you came and have been chosen to make the fullness of change in yourself which will also lift the world out of fallen nature.*

Our progression into The New World is not just a gradual increase of Light. This Zion is a different dimension with greater Light, even a thousand fold, and is governed by *principles* rather than rules and laws. The current kingdom you live in now is governed by these rules and commandments, which are referred to as the rule of *the Law and the Prophets*. This level rules with a hierarchy that places individuals over others. In the Zion Kingdom, every individual understands the principles which the rules and commandments of the lower Kingdom were based upon. Therefore, in Zion, people govern themselves by these principles. *Every person will know Me personally,* so I will work with each one by adding Light, which holds My Wisdom, even the Wisdom of the Father. I will work with you in the same way.

Zion is highly progressive. When you are in a Zion way, you do not work from limiting habits and patterns. The spirit of Zion has *newness* in every moment. You are aware of many righteous possibilities, choosing from your own preferences and uniqueness. You move forward acting on one possibility, then the next moment opens up with a wider understanding and a greater variety of possibilities.

When you are working still from *fallen nature* patterns and moving out of that distorted way, at first your choices seem to narrow as they move out of the impure. As I mentioned in a previous chapter, the choices will narrow as you begin to clarify what is *truth*. Yet, when coming from your true nature, the possibilities begin to *expand* until you are like God, whose possibilities of how to move forward are *infinite*. All of your ever-expanding possibilities and choices will bring you success, progression, more love, more joy, more peace, more understanding, more truth expressed through you and realized with the power to create and expand constantly.

A Higher Way, an Expansive, Freeing Way

A blessing sometimes is a blessing for a time, and then it is no more. It is a blessing to have a commandment as it serves to direct you. But as you progress, the commandment takes on a different way of being. First, it is a rule. It is very direct; it seems exact. There are many who want to teach their opinions of what that commandment means and how it was to be lived. A beautiful example of this is from the Ten Commandments that Moses brought forth. The people did not want to accept the freedom that was offered to them. They asked others to explain what keeping the Sabbath Holy means and how it is to be lived. Many rules were created until hundreds and eventually, even *thousands* of directions were given to tell the people how to obey the original commandments. But I am inviting you forward to understand a commandment in a new way.

A commandment is an invitation from God to come and co-create with Him. It gives you direction. When you understand the commandments in the higher way—the spirit and reason for the commandment—they are not so much a specific set of rules with limits, but they hold the *spirit and nature of working with God.* To work with Our wisdom is to experience the perfect knowing of what the Father and I have for you. *Let Me create with you.* We know how to open up many possibilities for you to make a new, optimum choice in each moment, different and better than yesterday. One situation is not exactly the same as another, but rather each circumstance is unique with different influencing factors. Come. Let Our Spirit be with yours. Let your spirit be more with Us that the day-to-day choices you make will be infused with the power of godliness and Our enhancement.

All this is extended to you because of the Atonement. I remind you: the spirit of commandment is the spirit of *creation*, not restrictions. If you were to tell children to be creative and then tell them exactly what to do, it would thwart their creativity and their ability to express, learn, grow, and develop. A child is free to create with these directions: *Here is a piece of paper. I would like you to look at all the beautiful colors. Look at the world and see all the beautiful things that are there. What is in your heart? What do you see? Put on this paper what you feel and what you see with all the beautiful colors you love the most.*

The directions to the child are like commandments. *Commandments are the Light of God, which I give to you from Love.* Our Light is poured forth to you through these commandments. They are to assist you to see the truth and a safe course to follow. They give clarity on the best way to move forward. With all the holy principles as your tools, you will be free to create beautiful things in your life. Our Love adds *life* to all you are creating in this world.

Be open to the beautiful directions that are not constricting, but freeing, opening, and expanding. Come let Us work with you—not to dictate, not to command in the old sense of the word, but to be *free*. See the principles that are involved. Like the parent with the child, I want you to notice the 'color of life' and which combinations are harmonious. For example, we might begin to teach you what 'green does' and when to use it. We will talk about the 'green' in your life that you might be more empowered to create harmony.

Surrendering into Greatness

I am here with you. God and the Heavens desire to work at your side, empowering, strengthening, adding on, *but not taking over.* Many think that 'surrender' means they must give up, not have a will of their own. If this were so, you would have no will, no choice, no desire, and no creative powers. *It is not so! That is not to be.* Your will, your agency and power to decide is a sacred gift God has given to you and will never take from you. There is a misunderstanding about surrendering one's will to God. This is *not* what is asked.

Surrendering to God means: *Submit your will (to 'turn it in', as you would submit a term paper). Let Him reveal to you His will (which is far vaster in knowing all things and holds His wisdom). Let His will expand yours, that you might see more variety, more possibilities in the Holy manner of how things can be created. Come and let your will and your desires be united with His and work with Us. Come and be with Us that We might create together.* We see far more expansively and will share with you all the possibilities in a pure and loving manner. Allow your will to join with God so His will and wisdom can join with yours. He will take your sacred will and gently hold it with His and then surround you with the greater. I will be there to deliver His will and make it known to you. I know how powerful this is from My own experience of submitting My will to the Father. *It is glorious!*

Though I had the attributes of Father in Me when upon the Earth, I did not have the *fullness* of His expanded power. When I submitted My will unto the Father in the Garden of Gethsemane, His greatness—even much greater than Mine—allowed the *fullness of all that He is* to explode into My being from the 'God-kernel' of Divinity placed in Me. This opened up in Me the full infinite potential of His power. Then I could understand His vast and infinite will. The release of full Godliness surrounded and empowered Me so that I could move forward to complete the Holy sacred Atonement. I was not giving up, even though many thought I was. *I was strengthened by My surrendering.*

Submitting My will to the will of the Father emboldened Me with the infinite strength I needed to complete My holy commission. You are also invited to surrender and submit to God for His expanding to take place in you. *Ultimately, surrendering your will to God expands you.* Come and co-create with God. Come and co-create your life, not in a replicated mold, but in the beautiful uniqueness you are developing. He desires for your individual, unique being to unfold out of the agency given to you from the beginning.

You are invited to understand the beauty of who you are. The creative power of God is within you. *The unfolding of your spirit's true nature is necessary to create Zion.* Part of this is the full realization that your unwanted patterns and unrighteous desires *are not you—not the true you.* They are fallen nature energies that you are experiencing in this world. This powerlessness is part of the lies and illusions of Satan's wiles and ploys. This energy force is actually within you for the time being, but you do not need to stay captive to its compulsions. Connecting your True Nature to Me does not bind you. With us, as a team, the binding ways can be released and be replaced with Godly ways. When joining with Me and gathering your faith with the Light and Love of the Father, you can let go of any negative, unrighteous patterns, and release your greatness and goodness, so you move forward each day in greater godly power.

When you begin obeying a commandment, you may feel a little restricted or overwhelmed similar to when you are first being trained in something new. When you are practicing artwork or learning a new skill, you must first master using the different instruments of the trade, which seem awkward in the beginning. Then, you become more proficient as you practice the techniques, and you can allow your spirit to freely express itself through the medium or skill you have chosen, creating many beautiful things. You are at the starting gate to have your creative powers develop and expand your godly talents. In the same way, as you practice obeying commandments, you will not feel constrained or intimidated by them. You are beginning to understand eternal principles and learning to govern yourself. I offer you the freedom to create goodness, godliness, Light, and Love, and move forward in every possible way.

Create with Me

Take up this expanded awareness which I keep mentioning. Come and work with Me. I know you have already heard this, and you might be saying: *Well, I have been working on this. Why do you keep saying this to me?* When you hear these Truths explained again in a clearer and deeper way, you will see a new level in what I am saying. Just keep moving forward. Keep praying more fervently, sincerely, and mightily from your whole soul. As you do so, your understanding will expand and keep expanding. The steps you make will be significantly larger. Your progression will compound, your abilities multiply, and momentum builds. The Light you and I increase will catapult you into a whole new dimension of learning and progressing. *You will catch the spirit of Zion.*

Remember, I have said that the powers and capacities are to be a thousand-fold more than in this current world. This is Zion, a whole new level and a whole new way of being, far beyond what you have comprehended. When you begin to experience what I am talking about to the degree I know it can be, the ability to move forward is huge in relationship to how you have progressed heretofore. You truly are to move forward in this expedited way, receiving the fullness of My Gift and be abundantly *Alive in Me.*

I am inviting you to develop this ability to *expedite* time, to move forward so you might accomplish much in *just a day*, a thousand fold from what you have before. Can you even imagine what it would be like to learn and accomplish in one day what you did in a thousand? Does this seem like an exaggeration or just a symbolic representation? *Come and find out; let Me prove this truth. It is not an exaggeration; it is a reality. Just start. It can be.* Learn to quickly change or improve patterns and become better and better and better and accelerate. There are so many wonderful ways to accomplish and create in a spiritual-energy enhanced way. I eagerly look forward to showing you. This is what you must have, and this time is very crucial because the time for the upward steep climb is to begin *now*.

Don't delay! Start today! *Stop and pray right now!* Literally, come pour your heart out in prayer. Set your intention to begin to practice what I am teaching in this book this very moment! Begin to release yourself from the fetters of timing, constraints of understanding, the limits of commandments, and the controls of others. When you begin to practice with Me at your side, you can quickly change and improve patterns twice as much as yesterday, then tomorrow four times more, then eight times and so forth. You may not always be aware of the growth, but it will be there. *Continue practicing!* The power begins to multiply, and the synergy takes place in you. I am here to open up a new realm and dimension of frequency for you, so you will be ready for all that is yet to come. We must create this new way, this new frequency, this new level of Light, even a Zion order, a Terrestrial world here upon the Earth—*and it begins in you.*

Open Awareness

I am saying this to you right now, so you might open up your mind and your awareness, which doesn't mean you have to work harder and faster—that is the old understanding. Open up to the power that comes not from the mind and the physical body alone, but a power from Me working in you. Changing and releasing old patterns will open you up. You will not hold on to habit, but each moment is fresh and new. You become free in Me, empowered, launched, moving forward, and expanding time in your life.

Ask Me to release all negative thoughts that say: *I can't. It does not work. It is too hard. I've tried this. I have to work harder and faster and more.* With such thoughts and feelings comes the mindset: *How can I ever? I am already doing a lot.* In a new way with Me, it's different. There is a lot more ease. Progress naturally happens. When you are in this new pattern, Light is working within you through the night. You awaken the next day with a natural increase of divinity in your subconscious. Then each moment, this new way becomes more a part of you, and you will become more conscious of the internal work I am doing in you. The next day you are calmer and wiser; you are more intelligent. You have more information to access, and this happened naturally throughout the night.

Did you work harder? No. Especially when fallen patterns are removed, your Divinity grows as naturally as the development of a baby. The baby makes efforts, this is true, but it is not a fight or battle. Even what may ap-

Chapter 15 – Developing the Zion Way

pear to be a struggle to the little one is just effort—and there is *joy* in the effort! In the same way, you can progress with your innate divinity, uninhibited by the destructive energies of the dark one. You move forward as God's Divinity naturally progresses in your physical body. I desire to give to you more of My Light in greater portions, allowing the Divinity within you to be fed by God's Love.

You are of God, the Eternal Father and the Holy Mother, and your innate, pure Divine Nature grows. You are to take on your full divinity. When you were first formed—though you were created out of Divine design—you did not have the fullness of Divine power. With Me, you are opening up to allow Divinity in you to expand, increase, empower, and change the very nature of the physical form until it becomes just as Divine as your spirit. *Godliness is the potential you hold.*

You are at the forefront of building this new world, a new way of life, our Zion. There is no evidence or examples of the many wonderful things that I have spoken of in the world today. *There are no examples in this world of the profound things I am talking about.* I am working with many right now to open up their minds to see My extended vision for this world and its inhabitants. I am inviting you forth to be among My leaders because you and I made a *covenant* to create this level of Divinity in you and the world at this time. Work with Me every day. *I am ready.*

Be aware of My presence as I stand right at your side. Father and I *are* there in energy and power. You have the *innate capacity* to be fully aware of Us every moment. Hold the thought of Me at your side so strong that you would turn and expect to see Me. Remember, I am with you giving you *all* the support, enhancement, enlightenment, empowerment for every moment always. *Expect miracles in your life as great as, or greater than, ever recorded in scriptures.*

See how to handle every situation as you accelerate in your growth and see what can happen in a 24-hour period. Experience a new freshness of possibilities. Again, there is not the old, only the empowering of the new, so that you come and co-create with Me powerfully every day. Then that power to create grows and builds in you, and you are not fettered by any of the old ways. You are greater than any of those.

It is true I say things many times, repeating everything again and again. I have always done this throughout all of time. *The repeat is necessary.* Like water on dry soil, a one-time watering will not make the soil wet enough to plant. The rains must continue to fall for the harvest to be abundant and the garden to be plush.

This is My message to you for now. You may at this point still be saying: *I still don't get just what I am to do. I still don't understand what the new way is.* Keep reading. In fact, it would be wisdom to *read this again even if you do think you understand.* Every time you sit down to read, begin with prayer. *Stop as you read an idea and ask Me to deliver the Light to quicken your understanding.* Ask to have a spiritual witness and gain a testimony.

Let My message grow in you. Be prayerful. *(I do believe I have said that before!)* There is a good reason I ask this so many times. Prayer is the absolute, *vital* key to working with Me. Exercise yourself in prayer. Step forward, for even one step starts to lay the foundation within you. *I speak Truth.* The Truth I speak connects to the Truth that is within you. When that connection takes place, you are raised and empowered to move forward.

Create the Foundation

Lay the foundation. Practice being more aware of Me. Notice the old patterns, and with Me, clearly set an intention to change for the better. Don't act from the same old habits; learn to live with Me with an *in-the-moment awareness* of options. Pray and set an intention to make every day even better than before. You will then be ready for the next chapter in your life. I will bring to you significant thoughts, which will move you forward from this world's current level of Light into the Zion realm. You will receive the fullness of My Atonement's power, My Gift of Eternal life for you—*your personal Eternal life.*

You are on the threshold of great things. Be in peace. Be grateful for the goodness that is developing within you. Express gratitude for *all* things in your life and in yourself, then express it again. Being in a state of gratitude makes you able to receive Light, more of Our power, Our

Love, Our appreciation, Our adoration of you, and Our joy in working and creating with you. For now, My dear precious one, I bring closure to this chapter, but not ever to Our connection.

Be aware and mindful. Ponder upon what I have presented, and it will enhance and expand you. Pray about these words. When you sleep, what I have spoken will begin to grow within you. By tomorrow this truth can have a positive influence on you. Let us move forward and give birth to Zion in this world by giving birth to Zion in *you*.

My Love to you personally.

Chapter 16
This Dispensation is Your Mission

My dear and precious friend, as you read this chapter I ask you to be in constant prayer. Now you might ask how it is possible to be reading and in prayer at the same time. You literally may ask your spirit to pray simultaneously as you are reading. I'd like you to be aware it is completely natural for your spirit to be actively engaged in a myriad of activities even as it continues to influence and direct your physical being. All this can be done while your mortal mind is focused on another topic. How wonderful! That holy part of you can offer the most sincere prayer from the center of your soul, producing a constant enlightenment in your being. Then, as you read, you will be more receptive in a completely new way. This will enable you to hear what I am saying with *expanded* understanding and with the *fullness* I have intended for you.

When I was upon this earth, I often gave My messages in parables, which had many meanings to them. I presented the material in this manner to teach at the various levels for that period or dispensation of time. This enabled Me to relate to each person's desire to learn and match their capacity to understand and live the teachings. Even if you do not understand the culture from which I drew My examples, the meanings of My teachings will still have the intended influence on you. *How is that?* As you are prayerful, the meanings can unfold. I do not speak in parables at this point, though sometimes I give you an analogy to help you further comprehend. *We must come out of the parable phase. It is now time to speak in an unveiled manner.* Our Zion must be built with transparent and unrestrained truth. Having your spirit in constant prayer will be beneficial to you, expanding your capacity anew. It is truly My desire at this point to be able to expand your level of knowledge and understanding as well as your ability to incorporate these teachings into your life.

Purposes of Dispensations
Let's talk about what this time frame on Earth is designed to accomplish. According to divine plan the earth has been carefully divided into periods of time with each one having a particular purpose. Our Heavenly Father has set an intention for each dispensation to disperse certain holy teachings. Every dispensation's purpose has built upon the foundation of the previous one. The prophets for each dispensation are those who have fulfilled that intention and have met all the requirements to rise to the fullness of the truths and teachings presented at that time. These righteous beings led beautiful lives and were excellent examples of living the holy truths presented to them. They were individuals who truly

Chapter 16 - This Dispensation is Your Mission

sought to know My will and the will of the Eternal Father. They were prayerful and *diligent* in communication with the Heavens and sought conscientiously for improvement in their personal lives.

Many good people have listened to and have followed the prophets. *This is the order and way of the first level of Light, the Telestial Kingdom of Glory.* The order of the 'Law and the Prophets' is vitally necessary to begin to establish a firm foundation for people to live righteously and come to God. This has been the basis of all dispensations up to this time. I am ready to lift a group of people to the next level, to the second level of Light, or Zion. This includes the Law and Prophets with the expansion of moving into principle-based living. *All Zion people will have the gift of prophecy and revelation, and each will learn to govern themselves.* I will draw these people closer to directly know Me. *You* are one of these because you are seeking further Light and Truth. I am asking you to seek Me even more diligently and experience communication with the Heavens.

The idea of the Atonement is not new. It has been around and spoken of even before I came into the world. However, with rare exception, it has been applied in a small measure relative to the vastness of the power that it possesses. I am preparing now to lift and transition *you* to the Zion, Terrestrial Light. This second level of Glory has the foundation of *working directly with Me.* I would have you remember, the mission of all prophets has always been to bring people to Me.

People who live in a particular time are given the opportunity to learn and live the intended teachings, purposes, and developments of their time frame. For example, the Law was emphasized in all the dispensations before I came to Earth. I brought mercy and Love to balance the Law. In the times that followed, these ruling elements became unbalanced again and the 'fullness' of the Love I brought was completely lost in the Dark Ages. *Laws ruled in extreme ways; there was no love.*

One vital mission in the current dispensation, the *Restoration Dispensation*, is to again restore the balance between Love and Law. There needs to not only be the balance but also *harmonious* interaction. This has not yet been fully achieved. The unity of Law and Love is still out of balance though some progress has been made. In this unbalanced state, Zion cannot come into fruition. *I am asking you to join with Me to remedy this.*

Though certain teachings are presented during a dispensation of time, no one is ever limited to the prominent truths of that time, but every person may always progress beyond the dispensation's purpose and intention. A good example of this is the great prophet, Enoch. He had a particular mission to fulfill by receiving, living, and teaching certain concepts. Enoch pursued far beyond what was intended for his dispensation. He not only kept asking for more understanding, he also kept developing greater righteousness in his life. He kept seeking intently for greater intelligence—more than I had sent for that dispensation. He believed being like God was the ultimate goal and kept focused on increasing in righteousness with the intent to glorify the Father. Not only did he receive the fullness of My Atonement's Gift, but he was also a powerful influence among the people of his city. He inspired and persuaded them to reach an exceptionally high level of living. This group of people was eventually lifted up, having their bodies changed and, therefore, not subject to death.

Current Dispensation's Unique Mission

There are two great intentions of the current dispensation, the *Dispensation of Restoration of the Fullness of Times.* The first mission is the restoring of all formerly revealed truths and Heavenly powers from the previous dispensations' main missions. A good portion of this is complete. The second objective is to fully restore Love with the Grace I brought, establishing the balance and fulfillment of the Law and all commandments. *Only* with My Love can there be the pure understanding of Law's purpose. *Only* with My Love can one actually live the Law.

The second purpose of the Restoration of the Fullness of Times cannot be completed by merely following the commandments. *I have begun to restore ordinances, powers, and additional knowledge.* I have also begun to restore the *Love.* There must be a *completion of My Divine Love* to fulfill the vital purpose I presented when I was on the Earth in My Dispensation of Grace. Many mistakenly believed I was attempting to *do away* with the Law. Instead, I came to *fulfill* or complete the Law's purpose.

The Law is to protect and give structure to the essence of Love, and Law must have Love to create life. This is the eternal way. I am now restoring the spirit, understanding, and unity of Law and Love to again *fulfill* the purpose of the Law and the Prophets. This completes the mission and the purpose for having commandments and prophets.

The timeframe right now is most unique. You are in a *transitional period* in which the Dispensation of Zion is overlapping with the Dispensation of Restoration. For those who come to Me, I have opened up the *spirit* of My new dispensation, with My *full* Love and Grace, the way it will be when I come again in Glory. In Me, this Glory holds the true balance and harmonizing of Love and Law. This Glory is available to those who have *allowed* the purpose of the Law and the Prophets to be fulfilled, and have come unto Me. *I will restore all purity as it was in Eden, expand Truth in full consciousness, and complete the glory intended for Earth.* The complete power and Truth of My millennial dispensation will be brought forth in fullness when I come again to dwell on Earth. *That time draws near.*

You need the spirit and teachings of My previous dispensation's Grace and Love to assist in the completion of both of these missions of the current Dispensation of Restoration. We must co-mingle this Dispensation's teachings with My Dispensation of Grace and Love. Let Me fulfill My role as Redeemer and teach you the higher

Chapter 16 - This Dispensation is Your Mission

revelations. Only in this way can the current truth being taught be nurtured by God's Love and become life-giving.

The fullness of Law cannot be successfully implemented into your nature until it is infused with *life*. This infusion only comes through My Love. This Love can only be fully given as you come to have a personal relationship with Me and know Me. Only Living Truth, *truth infused with Love*, will reveal My true purposes and the higher ways of living without misunderstanding. Only with Me will *you fully combine the new way—the way of Zion—with the Law and the Prophets.*

For what are the prophets sent to say? They say, *Here are the commandments and holy ways of God. Repent and come unto Christ, for only in Christ can you be saved.* You are asked to 'follow the prophet'. So what does the prophet do? He comes unto Me. He has a personal relationship with Me. He lives a righteous life through My Atonement. Follow the prophet's example and do likewise! People often come unto the prophets, but they stop there because they are *trying* to live in righteousness by keeping all the commandments. They do not let the purpose of the Law and the Prophets be fulfilled. The Law and the Prophets are only there to set a foundation of truth, a truth each one must choose to accept. However, *truth alone cannot save one.* Only with My power and My Love and Grace can you live in complete righteousness. This is the work the Father has sent Me to do.

You may wonder within yourself: *What is my personal purpose? What is my mission?* The very fact you are reading My message in this book is the first indicator that you are called to establish Zion. *The degree to which you are involved depends on your personal choice.* I will have a people—at least 144,000—who have, through My Grace and Love, overcome all of the fallen nature and at least begun living a Zion level of Glory. *I am offering this to you.* Please, progress with your commitment to continue climbing the mountain to higher lands. Come, take My hand; it is a *glorious* journey.

My Title Means Crystal
The name 'Christ' is one of the titles of My holy position. It is not actually My name, though I accept gladly when people call Me that. The word 'Christ', among other things, means crystal. This stone conducts light and diffuses a rainbow of colors. In a similar manner, I also diffuse words from the Light of Truth. It is this holy work I do that allows Me to be the communicative link between Heaven and Earth and serve as Mediator. Usually, when people are enjoying the crystal's beautiful rainbow, they are more focused on the colors rather than the stone's subtle energy. An actual power is produced by a crystal. Those who are sensitive to the crystal's energy can feel its radiating power. The crystal disperses light the way I disperse Truth. In the same way light moves through a crystal dispersing color, so does God's Light and Truth flow through Me dispersing principles and teachings. I love for you to enjoy the beautiful words—the beautiful color. However, even more than that, I desire for you to

Chapter 16 - This Dispensation is Your Mission

experience the wondrous power contained in what I deliver.

The Divine energy I distribute from My Soul and Being holds greater power than the words I bring forth. All of the words of Truth are combined together in Me, for I *am* The Word, which means the *wholeness* and the *completion of Truth*. I hold all Eternal Truth in perfect orderliness like the orderly array of the rainbow's colors.

This is the day to restore wholeness and oneness from all that has been scattered or given in parts. Now is the time to bring all the dispersed words and teachings back into Truth like the dispersed colors united back to a brilliant white light. *Receiving all of the understanding from earlier dispensations is necessary for you at this time of evolving.* The assignment at this time is to bring the commandments and teachings into a greater collective purpose and unified understanding, moving rules into *principles* which become part of your nature and everyday living.

Awaken the Passion

One of the greatest obstacles to overcome is the *disbelief in your personal divinity*. Many individuals have been so belittled in one way or another that they do not recognize their power and who they are. You may have looked at the prophets and holy men in past times and felt that they were somehow greater than you. They were not necessarily *greater*; it is more that they were very *diligent* in reaching out to the Heavens, to Me and God, the

Father. They received the holy words, studied them very intently, prayed mightily, and fasted for greater understanding as well as striving for excellence in implementing righteousness into their lives.

You are to be more *diligent* in gaining this greater understanding. However, just diligence will not suffice if you do so in the manner of just being obedient to the laws and just following the instructions to the letter of the law. Again, this way is of the first level of Glory, or the way the world has been at best. The prophets have been sent to lead people out of bondage from the fallen nature of sin and corruption.

Many live a portion of the commandments out of task and duty alone. Some of my diligent ones hunger and thirst to *know and understand* the teachings and scriptures. This is very good, but there is still more. I am inviting you to step up to your *maximum* capacity. Awaken to that deeper, more lasting fervor which is in you already. Most people have yet to experience a full releasing of their Love for God. This is the key. I ask you to come with the desire of your *whole* soul to naturally live righteously because you love the Truth and God. It is given for all to awaken to a much deeper righteousness, a oneness with Truth, and an infinite love for our Eternal God. *Only with Me can this be accomplished.*

Because of the standard and the ways of the world, you may have a tendency to be complacent about where and what you are. You may be satisfied or be brought into the

Chapter 16 - This Dispensation is Your Mission

illusion that where you are spiritually is acceptable. I'm not saying that it is not adequate for this moment. I am saying there is a deeper consecration and love that strongly exists in you; it is far beyond what you have ever experienced in this life. This depth of your own Love for the Divine can be reached now.

In the old pattern, you have believed that devotion means being more diligent in obedience: to do more, to work harder and make your life align with the commandments and the instructions. That will not reach this deep place within you. Often My very devoted ones work harder on listening to the directions, reading the scriptures, and outlining the lessons. They are trying to use their mind, their will power, and their diligence to accomplish a higher way of being and coming unto Me. This doesn't work for the greater way of living the Zion way of life. This way will not get you where you can go and what can be accomplished. It is *backwards* compared to the holier way.

Let Me explain further. When you reach the deep divinity within you and your Love for God, all of the 'proper behaviors' fall naturally into place. You do not need to *make* yourself do anything because righteous behavior is already within your spirit. Righteous behaviors flow from the center of your soul without compulsion or struggle.

In contrast, when you hold to a rule by obedience or *discipline* alone, like being honest for example, you might have a challenging situation in which you are tempted to not tell the truth. The mind could easily reason that it is a small matter in this case. The mind could also justify: *It isn't really breaking the rule, or it doesn't really matter.* In living by obedience to the laws or rules only, it is through one's discipline and the mind alone that decisions are made. So if the mind can find a *logical* reason to be dishonest, it will. In many teachings of the world, the mind is the origin of creation and the ruling force—the ultimate decision maker and creator. In that way of reasoning, the mind's intelligence and power can become a false god to follow and worship.

But I say to you, the mind is *not* the origin of the power to create, and intelligence is not your god. Your mind, with its intelligence, is along the pathway of creation and is an important part, but *the power to create originates from God and flows through your divinity—your true, godly nature.* Even My power to create originates from The Father. With your spirit's innate power of Love and Truth combined with My power as the Christ, with God's Light and with My *resonance* of Love, together we create from the true Origin of Creation. Every word I speak, even in this written form, is delivered with the power of Light, Love, and Truth. I want My vibration and your vibration to connect. Then that power from the Divine Parents, delivered through Me, naturally connects to the spiritual being that you are. *In this holy manner, you and I will create.*

Chapter 16 - This Dispensation is Your Mission

A Core of Pure Love

This divine nature within you holds experiences of deep love for your Eternal Parents, yet it is not fully awake because it is covered up. This is partly because of your being too busy with activities and also making efforts to meet the needs and requests from others. Beautiful, good works are definitely part of your life, but when your performances come only from the rules, your obedience to the instructions, or pleasing others, it can be a lower way of living. However, when you hold to the vibration and the Word that I am, the wholeness of the power of Light, Truth, and Love will expand the connection to your Origin, Our Eternal Parents, and reveal your true, divine nature. *At the core, you are pure Love.*

I bring forth the holy perfection of the Eternal Parents: Their greatness, Their perfection, Their wholeness, and Their infinity. I resonate and radiate Truth that touches and awakens that sacred part of you. Right at this moment, you can understand all I am saying to you on a deeper level, more than the understanding of your mind. Let your understanding be deep in every part of your being in which your whole soul understands and will awaken the power of the Love that you hold within you. This passionate, beautiful Love you have will surge out of your divine nature's core into your physical being, released by our frequent and daily connection.

You will feel this Divine Love in your physical body as it awakens new understandings, even on a constant basis. *Every day and every moment new ideas pour into you that you have not studied or gathered by reason alone, but by a natural unfolding of the divinity in you.* Then you will have the 'lights going on' because of the Light from within. This Truth is not weakened by the fracturing into different aspects, but its *wholeness* illuminates your entire being and impacts all that you do. This natural divinity and beautiful Love will be manifested in your life so powerfully that *anything* you need will be there.

Miracles
Prophets and righteous individuals have commanded the elements and brought forth miracles by tapping into the deep divinity within; their zeal for Divine and for Truth had been awakened. The ability of their beings had been developed to such a degree that Divine power could flow through them so that inspired proclamations manifested miracles. Miracles are the manifestation of My Light and Divinity in a person. I intend for this to be the same way for you as you steadfastly continue in the course I have prepared for you. As you receive My Gift and walk your highest path, the potential for miracles can be present every moment.

When you launch upon a direct, unwavering course to have your spirit and physical beings be united with Me, you may or may not experience 'miracles' seen with the outward eye or evidenced in the outward world. *The greatest first miracle to seek for is the complete cleansing of fallen nature from your physical being and the awakening of your spirit.* Now is the time for you to be 'born again' which is a state of holiness that *begins* the unity of

Chapter 16 - This Dispensation is Your Mission

your physical being with your true nature. Tapping into the connection to your eternal-self brings you to always be empowered by Divine.

It is one thing to have your being cleansed of all the nature of Satan, whose nature is devoid of any Love and His ways are all distorted in some manner. My Atonement has two parts that act to lift you to your true, divine nature. One is to cleanse all the attachments to fallen nature—the *false* ideas and *distorted* energies. Truth then becomes clear, and you sense how to respond honorably with the spirit of Truth in all situations. Second is the greater establishment of a certain level of Divine Love to match and empower the Truth you do know. Both of these parts are of equal importance and must be sought for. After the initial cleansing, there must still be the filling of your whole being with ample Love. This must also be maintained by continual daily prayer to keep you sufficiently filled with this holy Essence of Divine Love. To be kept alive in this greater state—a state which does not deteriorate—there must be ample, continual progression with our association and interaction. I am here to continue to feed your newborn being. *Then* we have the foundation for miracles.

In this holy state, Truth and Love become such a part of you that you only act in righteousness and in alignment with Divine's will. Relationships cease to be frustrating, annoying, or perplexing. You *automatically* and righteously respond in a loving nature in every circumstance. Your emotions do not have to be monitored; they are holy and divine. Sincerity is in you, and you live from your whole soul. My Light and Love dwell actively with you on a constant basis with awareness of My presence. Now, in every moment, you are *Alive in Me.* Come to the awakening of your full divinity, the power and passion and love that you are. *This is the first and greatest true miracle.*

As you advance in this 'born again' state, you will learn to do and create only by the will of the Father. You will stay in a constant power of knowing God's Will with a capacity to deliver and bring to pass His Will. Then you will witness True Miracles which can only take place with the extended power of God and are beyond the natural laws of this world.

Chapter 17

Prayer of the Spirit

Holy, sincere prayer is the sacred place to begin. Most people pray from the reasoning of their minds and the emotions of their physical being. This is why I have asked you to invoke your spirit to begin the prayer. You may ask: *How do I do that?* Simply say: *My spirit, come forth and say this prayer. My mortal mind is stepping back for you, my spirit, to lead my life.* I would that you experience the 'prayer of your whole soul' and begin to communicate from your spirit, not just from your mind and physical being. After a while, it will be automatic that all your prayers are from your spirit's center. The moment will come when your physical being will need to *completely* surrender any control so that you can pray from your spirit and the center of your soul. Pray for this surrender, asking Me to help in this. I will arrange experiences to prepare you for it. Stay with your efforts to ask your spirit to pray and lead your life; the fruits will come and be sweet.

We do hear, accept, and respond in some manner to all prayers. Those prayers involving all your faculties create a stronger condition in you to *receive* Our response.

When you are in mighty prayer, every part of your being is alert at that moment, and every cell seems to vibrate and be involved. There is a depth and a passion to what you're saying as you call out to God. Often mentally fervent or emotionally charged prayers are a cry for help to an intense situation or need. If your prayer is a request-driven prayer, that's good—but there is a more powerful way to pray.

A more powerful prayer is one that accesses your innate passion to express love to your holy Heavenly Parents. In a prayer of adoration and love, passion is invoked by accessing the deepest, purest part of you. Your passion doesn't come from a desperate need but from the depth of your awakened love for God. This is the most powerful way to pray and will do more to arouse your being and connect you to the Holy Mother and Eternal Father. Awaken that desire to open up your immense divinity and deep love from the center of your being, your holiness from the Mother and Father, and let *power* arise from your love and flow to your holy Parents.

Every time you pray I am also praying to God with you. These prayers of praise are the holiest of prayers. This is also what creates the most powerful communication with Me. I love the holy Eternal Parents in perfection! I am *alive* in that passionate and eternal love for Them which expands constantly! This holiest of love for the Divine is also within you and is what I desire to have fully awake and alive in you. All testimony of Truth is contained in the expression of this pure Love for our Eternal

Parents. You feel it; sometimes that feeling is quiet and still, soft and subtle, strong and powerful.

There is a form of life that you have not experienced yet. It is the power of the release of your divinity at its peak with your love of Truth and the Holy Ones, so powerful you will surge with the newness of the vitality in your divinity. The miracle of your power can be released in every moment, in every circumstance. Come to know the spirit of pure praise.

Humility and Fasting

There is true humility deep in your divine nature. *It is not arrogance to acknowledge the honesty of who you are.* Connecting to your true self is very humbling, and at the same time, it is very exhilarating and empowering as you step into this absolute honesty of self. It is unrighteous to be in pride or to exalt oneself, but it is also unrighteous to diminish or deny who you are. To gain the true spirit of humility, fasting is beneficial. For some individuals, fasting can support the stilling of the mind and quieting of the body. For others, fasting, at first, could be a delay, a distraction, or interference, but this will change in time.

The true spirit of fasting is *a quieting of the needs of the body so that the fervor and wholeness of your soul might shine forth.* When a person has not fasted before, it may be difficult at the beginning, but that does not necessarily mean that this is not a valuable tool for you, a way that you might *enhance your spirituality.* If fasting is new for you or has been difficult in the past, have several shorter fasts to prepare the body. If your body has a physical condition which does not tolerate going without food, plan to 'fast with food'. To do this, let your meals be simple, and the foods in their purest state. Let there be the minimum amount needed and, if possible an elimination of snacks. Also pray more often during your fast, no matter what the duration is. Prayer coupled with fasting gives a deeper purpose to the fast.

True fasting shifts the body from being nourished by food to being nourished by the Divine Light. Ask in prayer that your physical body is fed and blessed to gain nutrition and vitality from Spirit-Light. Your body can be trained to receive this beautiful Love that will nourish you. You can become more *alert* and *alive* with fasting. That is when your strength comes from your Holy Parents Divine Light and Love. Their strength supports you in awakening the powers within. Fasting is a way to increase the connection to the Holy Parents and to the magnificence of your spirit. Your whole soul that holds the divinity within will begin to awaken into a greater capacity.

The Miracle of the Quiet Place
Take less thought of how the miracle will be manifested, what it will look like or feel like. Instead, feel your divinity and the love that you have for Truth and your Divine Parents. Let your love be focused with praise, adoration, and gratitude; miracles and gifts will follow. Believe that My Atonement Gift is for *you* through mighty prayer and

mighty communication. Exercise yourself in that by asking your spirit and then coming to a quiet place.

Find a quiet place for this holy communication. Set aside the world, give adequate time. Remember to ask your spirit to also pray. Your ability will grow to access the sacred, reverent, stillness of being in the hallowed presence of Divine. As you speak My name and through My power, you will increase the ability to be aware of My presence and the presence of God. In time, your spiritual senses will heighten so that you will *feel* and *experience* the Love and Divine presence right at the beginning of the prayer. When the Divine ones are present, you will be keenly aware of them, and the desires within you for righteousness will increase tremendously. Yes, you are hungry for food and thirsty for water, but at the very same moment you are being fed with the *Bread of Life* and your thirst quenched with *Living Waters*.

As you really listen to what I have given to you, pray by saying: *My spirit, begin to pray mightily for me from the depths of my greater self.* Then invoke Me to pray with you: *Holy Mother and Father, in the name of Christ . . .* Oh, I will be there. I will be there with all of My Love, praying with you.

I would that you carefully re-read all that I have put forth previously and that you 'listen' to the words with your whole being, always allowing your spirit to bring forth that prayer so that you might hear and receive the vibration of Truth that I radiate to you. *That you not only see the variety of words like the full spectrum of color but that you feel the Light in your being.* Then, in My position as the Christ, the Crystal, the Mediator for Light from the Divine Holy Ones above, I will connect the center of your soul's divinity to Eternal Life. This sealed connection can be accomplished while upon the earth in your physical body. When the infusion comes forth, your body, literally, will be so illuminated that your Light will shine, and you will be alive, oh, so fully *Alive in Me!* This is what I ask you to do.

Preparing for a Blessing
Now, at this point, I ask you to prepare for a blessing I desire to give to you through this book. Begin with a prayer before you start to read the blessing. Ask that you might receive a testimony of all I have given to you. When you read the blessing, imagine that I am standing just a bit above you and slightly to your right side, for I will come in spirit and place one hand over the crown of your head and the other hand over your heart. Because you will be reading the blessing—though I will speak the words anew—read each line carefully and then close your eyes and ponder on the words you have just read, hearing them over again in your mind as much as you can remember. *Feel the energy of my blessing as much as you have the capacity at this time.*

Whenever you choose to read and receive this blessing again, it will grow and be more powerful. An optimum would be to receive this blessing every day for 40 days. It will make a significant difference in your ability to grasp all I am presenting to you, and your ability to take strides forward to work with Me. Let Me lift your life to a level of Love and Truth greater than you have ever had before.

Oh, I do desire to deliver the wholeness and touch the power in you. If there is the slightest doubt or thought that diminishes or dilutes anything that I have said, ask for that to be washed away. Do not think these are 'only words'. Speak boldly and clearly saying: *In the name of Jesus, My Christ, I release fears and worries and dismiss all doubts and reservations. I step in with faith to claim the blessing in Light that my Lord is ready to give to me right now!*

You have the opportunity to have a precise, truly powerful, spiritual experience. This is sacred time right now if you will allow it to be. In this moment be sincere, be open and ask. It is My desire to send My Light and Love into you as if the whole of Me stood beside you pouring My Light vitality into you so that My virtue unites with yours. We can have this experience right now. I know some of you think that you will do this later. *Please do so now!* Or as soon as you can make the quiet time to do so. Take time for prayer. Have your own personal prayer now. When you have finished, open your eyes and read—I will spiritually be there to give you this blessing.

A Blessing from the Lord

With My Love, oh, holy, dear, precious child, I wash you with My Light—I bless you with My Living Waters to come now and fill you—I bless you to choose to release the patterns of the world—I bless you to have your unwanted ways washed away now—I bless you to receive the fullness of My Atonement as you seek for such—I fill you with My Light and Truth to touch the center of your Truth—

Receive now all holy knowing that it might fill your being—Awaken fully and arouse your faculties, both spiritually and physically—Completely believe the Truth that you are a child of God... a divine being... of infinite worth—I send the vibration of Who I am into you now—I fill you with the pure Love I have for you, who thou really art—My Love is now touching the love in you—I touch the center place within you wherein your spiritual zeal and the wholeness of your soul exists.

Feel this beautiful, physical tabernacle that is your body, even a temple body—I bless you with gratitude and love for this body—I bless you with Light to nourish this body until the fullness of life within is in every particle of your being—I bless you with the fullness of life to be completely expressed in this physical body—I thin the veil in you to allow the stirring of your inward soul.

Open now and feel the closeness of your Holy Mother and Holy Father—I bless you to feel Their Presence—I bless you to remember who you are and feel who you are without restraint—I bless you to remember our relationship and the Love of your Holy Parents—I bless you to bring forward into present time in your life, the open connection to Heaven—Come, Light Being that you are, for I bless you to continue to open up until there is no more veil—I bless you that this may always remain with you and grow and increase according to your choosing.

I bless you that these words filled with My Light will be manifested and expressed in you—I bless you with My Love, for it is pure and specific for you—Receive the Love of your Heavenly Mother and your Heavenly Father which I send into you—Receive Us now, and We will rejoice forevermore—I praise Our Holy Parents and seal this blessing upon you—I give this blessing with My Love and in the Name of the Holy, Eternal Mother and Eternal Father. Amen.

Final Remarks - Concluding Request

Oh, precious child of God, eternal one, come closer, my dear one. You have read my words; let them be heard again and again in your inner being. Pray again, even with Me, and I will bless this message to grow within you. Return many times to hear Me again through these words I have sent unto you.

When you feel a need to have an answer, when you are blocked or frustrated or feel distant from any help or answer, come read again. Come in prayer and ask to be guided, and I will lead you to the place in this book that will give you answer, guidance, and hope. I will open the words to show you the understanding that you need, the power to move forward, and the peace to walk calmly in the storms that will yet be.

Let this book be a meeting place where you and I will gather together again, and I will open these words to be heard anew with greater Light, expanding in your being each time you read. Hold this book in your hands, hold it next to your heart and feel Me close to you for I am in the book. *These words are of Me, and I will draw you closer to Me and our Holy God.*

Final Remarks - Concluding Request

This is My blessing to you now. Receive it and Know and feel you are My precious child, too.

Jesus, the Christ

Alive in Christ – *The Gift*

Paragraph Headings Index

A New Way 167
All Truth Is Connected 149
All Virtues and All Truth Will Expand in You 94
Ascending of Great Beings for this Earth's Boost 30
Awaken the Passion 197

Becoming Aware 162
Becoming One with Us 52
Begin Now 35
Being *Alive in Christ* 2
Being Away for Learning 59
Blessing from the Lord 212
Born Again 5
Born into Greater Glories 28
Bring the Two Worlds into Unity 136
Bypassing Diversions 107

Clarifying Your Responsibility 120
Come, I Will Take You Unto Them 98
Coming to Oneness 140
Consistency, Increase, Gratitude, and Praise 21
Constant Peace, Joy, and Hope 58
Core of Pure Love 201
Create the Foundation 187
Create with Me 182
Current Dispensation's Unique Mission 193

Developing Your Spiritual Awareness 104
Divine Eternal Source 85
Divine Eternal Substance of Love 82
Down Side to Habits 166

Embrace Life Fully 77
Embrace New Patterns 168
Essence of Love and Truth 112
Experience Your Spirit Self 49

Faith in Communication 42
Fed and Energized from Two Different Sources 84
Feeling the Presence of God's Spirit 80
Final Remarks - Concluding Request 214
Finding True Guidance 164
Five Significant Aspects 170
Future New World 34

Higher Way, an Expansive, Freeing Way 176
Holy Order of Things 55
Holy Sacred Space Beyond Words 117
How Long Will It Take? 150
How You Multiply Spiritual Energy 87
Humility and Fasting 207
Humility and Surrendering to God's Will 76

I Am Asking You to Be Vulnerable 137
Impressions Sent To You by Heavenly Beings 106
Inspired Living 19

Know Me-Know Truth 157

Let Me Become Your Prophet 138
Life Plan Reality on Earth 73
Life Plans and Resurrection 64
Live in Continual Peace, Joy, and Love 122
Living Testimony 143

Maintain the Love Factor 109
Making It Part of Your Nature 151
Making These Truths Your Nature 40
Meaningful Spiritual Experiences 27
Miracle of the Quiet Place 208
Miracles 202
Misunderstandings 10
More Alive! 131
My Invitation for You 95
My Invitation to You 129
My Request 101
My Title Means Crystal 196

Now is the Day for Acceleration 134

On Earth as it is in Heaven 91
Open Awareness 184
Open Up Your Eyes 142
Opposing Forces 60
Other Death Phenomenon 66
Overcoming Death for the New World 71

Physical Death, Life Review, and Resurrection 65
Power of Decision 124
Power of Spirit in Words 46
Preparing for a Blessing 210
Purposes of Dispensations 190

Quickened Resurrection 67

Restoring Divine Peace 51

Sacred Prayer Time 37
Second Birth, Second Glory 29
Spirit of Victory 172
Surrendering into Greatness 179

The Awakening 44
The Part the Mind Plays 41
The Thinking and the Doing 45
Then Nothing Can Take Your Life! 155
Third Birth, Third Glory 29
Truth Replacing the False 31
Two Sources for Learning 135

Unifying the Spirit with the Physical Body 6
Using Subtle Energy 108

Value of Sacred Time 17

Walk Forward in Prayer 57
What You Have Not Heard-What You Have Not Seen 118
Working with Christ and His Redeeming Power 62

Your Being is to Be a Portal to Heaven 92
Your God-Given Birthright 141
Your Spirits Vital Desire 154
Your Ultimate Physical Body 133